Maximizing Self-Reflections in the Classroom

What if we could guide children to self-reflect on their level of understanding, to learn what concepts they truly grasp and to identify those concepts with which they still struggle—before and after being assessed on these concepts? What if they could take this information and produce a plan to help themselves master material before an assessment? This practical book will enable you to work with students more effectively so they can evaluate their own levels of understanding, and determine strategies to get them from where they are academically to where they need to be. You'll also find out how to involve families, since self-reflection works better when students, teachers, and families partner in the learning process. Appropriate for K-8 teachers and curriculum coordinators, the book is perfect for teamwide book studies and teacher training. Examples are included throughout, and the appendix tools can be downloaded for classroom use.

Ellen Richard taught several grades as an elementary classroom teacher, earned her Gifted/Talented endorsement, and now works as a math interventionist in grades K-6.

Also Available from Routledge Eye On Education
(www.routledge.com/k-12)

Creating, Grading, and Using Virtual Assessments: Strategies for Success in the K-12 Classroom
Kate Wolfe Maxlow, Karen L. Sanzo, and James R. Maxlow

Rigor and Assessment in the Classroom
Barbara R. Blackburn

Passionate Learners: How to Engage and Empower Your Students
Pernille Ripp

20 Formative Assessment Strategies that Work: A Guide Across Content and Grade Levels
Kate Wolfe Maxlow and Karen L. Sanzo

Better Questioning for Better Learning: Strategies for Engaged Thinking
Benjamin Stewart Johnson

12 Characteristics of Deliberate Homework
Erik Youngman

Maximizing Self-Reflections in the Classroom

Enhancing Learning for Students, Teachers, and Parents

Ellen Richard

Routledge
Taylor & Francis Group
NEW YORK AND LONDON

Cover image: © Getty Images

First published 2023
by Routledge
605 Third Avenue, New York, NY 10158

and by Routledge
4 Park Square, Milton Park, Abingdon, Oxon, OX14 4RN

Routledge is an imprint of the Taylor & Francis Group, an informa business

Library of Congress Cataloging-in-Publication Data
Names: Richard, Ellen, author.
Title: Maximizing self-reflections in the classroom : enhancing learning for students, teachers, and parents / Ellen Richard, M.Ed.
Description: New York, NY : Routledge, 2023. | Includes bibliographical references. | Identifiers: LCCN 2022019554 | ISBN 9781032358826 (hardback) | ISBN 9781032325170 (paperback) | ISBN 9781003329176 (ebook)
Subjects: LCSH: Reflective teaching. | Reflective learning. | Language arts (Elementary)--Activity programs. | Language arts (Middle school)--Activity programs. | Mathematics--Study and teaching (Elementary)--Activity programs. | Mathematics--Study and teaching (Middle school)--Activity programs.
Classification: LCC LB1025.3 .R5342 2023 | DDC 371.102--dc23/eng/20220708
LC record available at https://lccn.loc.gov/2022019554

ISBN: 978-1-032-35882-6 (hbk)
ISBN: 978-1-032-32517-0 (pbk)
ISBN: 978-1-003-32917-6 (ebk)

DOI: 10.4324/9781003329176

Typeset in Palantino
by SPi Technologies India Pvt Ltd (Straive)

Access the Support Material: www.routledge.com/9781032325170

Dedicated with love to my parents, who were my first and best teachers, and to my amazing husband, who supports and encourages me always.

Support Material

The Appendix templates in this book will also be available on our website as free downloads, so you can easily print and reproduce them for classroom use. To access them, go to the book product page at www.routledge.com/9781032325170 and click on "Support Material."

Contents

*Note from the Author—the student work samples in this guide are based loosely on actual student work, but have been recreated and changed for clarity.

Meet the Author

Ellen Richard, MEd. earned a Bachelor of Science degree from the University of Notre Dame in Notre Dame, Indiana and a Master of Education in Early Education degree from Marymount University in Arlington, Virginia. She taught several grades as an elementary classroom teacher, earned her Gifted/Talented endorsement and now works as a math interventionist in grades K-6. She took time away from teaching to stay home with her four beautiful children, Katie, Susie, John and Emma.

Acknowledgments

I am so very thankful to my ever-optimistic and encouraging husband, Steve. I could not have written this book without your support.

I would like to thank my mom, Lynn—a gifted educator—for taking the time to read this text and offer her valuable insights.

Thanks to my beautiful children and dear family members for cheering me on as I begin this new chapter of my life. I appreciate your encouragement so much.

1

Significance and Philosophy

"You don't know what you don't know" is an old adage thrown around frequently. However, I believe that often times, students **do** know what they don't know, especially when they are given coaching and opportunities to reflect on their levels of understanding. What if we could guide our students to reflect on their own level of understanding, to learn to realize what concepts they truly grasp and what concepts with which they still struggle—before and after being assessed on these concepts? What if they could take this information and come up with a plan to help themselves master material before an assessment? Valle, Andrade, Palma, and Hefferen (2016) explain that

> [s]elf-assessment is meant to give students an opportunity to take control over their learning by having them assess gaps in their own understanding and skills, and then use what they learn about their strength and weaknesses as feedback for closing those gaps.

With proper practice and guidance, students of all ages and ability levels can learn to reflect on their own levels of understanding, and then parents, teachers and the students themselves can use that information to maximize learning. I believe that we owe our students a chance to self-reflect on their level of understanding at different times in the continuum of learning and assessment.

DOI: 10.4324/9781003329176-1

As educators and parents, we must be willing to work with our students to help them learn to evaluate their own levels of understanding, **and** determine strategies to get them from "where they are" academically to "where they need to be." How many times have you wondered how a student could test so poorly after you, the teacher or the parent, worked so hard with the child on the content at hand? How often has a student said that they don't have any questions about the material and then missed related questions on a test? How many times have you wondered if you were wasting time teaching something that the child already knows? Is the strategy you are using effective at getting a child to master the concept? What else do you need to focus on to help the student master the concept at hand?

Quite simply, this guide is intended to help teachers, students and parents work together to maximize student success by asking students to reflect on their true level of content understanding at various points in the learning process, namely before being assessed, after the assessment takes place (but before it has been evaluated), and finally after the assessment has been evaluated. Determining where each student is (in terms of understanding), where they need to go and the best route for them to take to master their objective(s), are critical steps toward educational success, and are most easily achieved when student, teacher, and parent are working together (see Figure 1.1).

We've known for years that assessment is absolutely essential to good teaching. Teachers, parents and students need assessment to gauge student comprehension and mastery of material. Can the student show mastery of the skill at hand, or is further instruction needed? Is the student ready to move on or build on, or is there a gap in understanding? Without a solid foundation, students' long-term academic success is at risk of collapsing as more and more content is piled on. And, of course, assessment is one integral piece of the puzzle that allows teachers, parents and students themselves to measure student mastery. In this guide, I assume that all teachers will use some form of summative assessment—whether it be paper/pencil, multiple choice, performance-based or any other format—to gauge student understanding.

The method for which assessments are used to determine understanding is changing, though. No longer is assessment analysis just for teachers, nor is analysis of any kind reserved solely for a post-assessment period. **Students, teachers, and parents are quickly learning that the most beneficial effect of assessment comes when they all work together, before, during and after an assessment.** Students must be able to clearly identify and share what they do and do not understand before, during and after an assessment, teachers must know exactly where their students are on the spectrum of

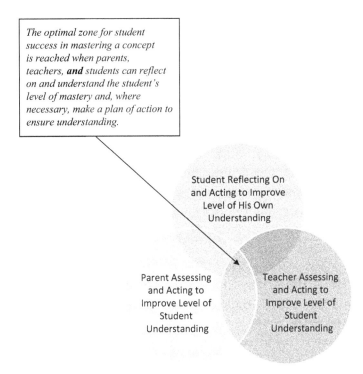

*The optimal zone for student success in mastering a concept is reached when parents, teachers, **and** students can reflect on and understand the student's level of mastery and, where necessary, make a plan of action to ensure understanding.*

Student Reflecting On and Acting to Improve Level of His Own Understanding

Parent Assessing and Acting to Improve Level of Student Understanding

Teacher Assessing and Acting to Improve Level of Student Understanding

Figure 1.1 Student, parent, and teacher working together.

The optimal zone for student success in mastering a concept is reached when parents, teachers, and students can reflect on and understand the student's level of mastery and, where necessary, make a plan of action to ensure understanding.

understanding, and, ideally, parents are also willing and able to help their children close any gaps that exist before or after assessments.

Role of the Student: Reflect on level of conceptual understanding, determine and implement a viable and effective plan of action to fill in any "gaps"; reflect on and demonstrate mastery of skill or objective

Role of the Teacher(s): Teach and guide student to practice self-reflection; assist student in successfully completing the plan of action needed to achieve mastery; reflect on effectiveness of remediation or support by looking at trends in individual and whole-class mastery or misconceptions, and determine the cause if there are continued issues

Role of the Parent(s): Encourage student self-reflection; support student's plan of action; communicate with teacher to share insights or ask for additional resources; follow up with student to check progress and mastery

This model of student self-reflection brings parent, students and teachers together in a constructive way that allows them to all work together to maximize student success. In her article, titled "Self Assessment for Understanding," McDonald (2007) explains that, "[t]eachers and students become partners in the process of assessment and self directed learning." I would add that this model of pre-assessment and post-assessment student self-reflection offers parents several opportunities at different points in time to also join in on their child's educational journey. Undoubtedly, those three parties (student, teacher, and parent) working together form the most solid foundation for student achievement.

This guide's utility is most fully realized when teachers, students and parents take active roles in gauging student understanding **both before and after assessments** take place. Students need assessments to understand their own strengths and weaknesses. Likewise, teachers can determine a student's level of understanding by analyzing assessment results. And, finally, parents can benefit their children greatly by analyzing assessment results to tease out what it is their children already know and what still needs to be mastered. However, in addition to evaluating results *after* an assessment takes place, I believe students need the opportunity to reflect on their understanding *before* an assessment occurs. In fact, they need an opportunity to gauge their understanding with enough time before the assessment takes place to allow teachers, parents and themselves opportunities to remediate if necessary. That way, when the formal assessment takes place, students' chances for success are maximized. According to the Common Core Standards, "With students, parents, and teachers all on the same page and working together for shared goals, we can ensure that students make progress each year and graduate from school prepared to succeed in college and in a modern workforce" (http://www.corestandards.org/the-standards).

Figuring out what students know and don't know makes a huge difference for which concepts are planned at the beginning of a unit, how long a unit needs to last, which concepts require remediation, and, in many instances, what trends of (mis)understanding are showing up in entire classrooms. **Helping students, teachers and parents understand and pinpoint students' levels of understanding before, during and after each assessment—and then adapting teaching styles, study habits and content accordingly—is the purpose of this guide.**

Furthermore, according to the Common Core Math Standards:

Mathematically proficient students start by explaining to themselves the meaning of a problem and looking for entry points to its solution. They analyze givens, constraints, relationships, and goals. They make conjectures about the form and meaning of the solution and plan a solution pathway rather than simply jumping into a solution attempt. They consider analogous problems, and try special cases and simpler forms of the original problem in order to gain insight into its solution. They monitor and evaluate their progress and change course if necessary (CCSS.Math.Practice.MP1, http://www.corestandards.org/Math/Practice)

While this quotation was written with math as the focus, there is no reason to limit the practice of student self-reflection to just math. For all subject areas, students should be told the target objectives, and given time to reflect on their own levels of understanding of each objective. Then, they need to formulate—and execute—a strategic plan to fill in any gaps and finally, reflect again on whether or not they have mastered the skill(s). If they have proved mastery, they are ready to move on. If not, the process repeats. McDonald (2007) remarks that "this kind of [self] assessment develops feelings of ownership and responsibility for learning and assists students in becoming independent learners who develop control over their own learning."

I created these pre- and post-assessment student self-reflection templates because I feel that having students write (or draw, type or verbally explain, etc.) their thinking about the unit of study before, during, and after they are assessed on it—no matter what the content area—helps to record this proficiency or lack thereof. Reflection of one's own understanding is a skill that must be taught, practiced, and reviewed. Having students write down their thinking can help students themselves, parents and teachers understand the student's thinking and processes better.

As an experienced elementary teacher in a high-risk, low-income school, I have learned several things:

- ◆ maximizing every teaching moment is critical;
- ◆ most students in the elementary and mid-level grades do not know how to "study" for tests when teachers ask them to do so;
- ◆ most children are honest about what they do and do not already know *when there is a solid rapport established between the individual student and teacher*;

◆ parents can and should be active participants in helping their children master different concepts, but often do not know how to go about doing so;

◆ teachers often misunderstand the true root of poor grades, many times blaming individual student's lack of effort or ability, rather than analyzing class-wide trends to determine the efficacy of their own teaching; and

◆ student self-assessments can make a teacher's job easier and more efficient since the student is helping to identify and remediate his own areas weakness both pre- and post-assessment

There are myriad research papers praising the value of student self-assessment. (For this text, I intend "self-reflection" and "self-assessment" to be used interchangeably; however, I rely more on the former so as not to be confused with references to pre- and post-assessments, like tests, quizzes, performance tasks, essays, etc.) McMillan and Hearn (2008) state that:

> Correctly implemented, student self-assessment can promote intrinsic motivation, internally controlled effort, a mastery goal orientation, and more meaningful learning. Its powerful impact on student performance—in both classroom assessments and large-scale accountability assessments—empowers students to guide their own learning and internalize the criteria for judging success.

McMillan and Hearn (2008) continue by saying that through self-assessment, "students identify their learning and performance strategies, provide feedback to themselves based on well-understood standards and criteria, and determine the next steps to enhance their performance." In short, student self-reflections, both before and after assessments, can encourage and empower students to take control of their own learning. The students are tasked with identifying their own weaknesses, determining a plan to improve their understanding, and then reflecting on how well they accomplished their objective. McMillan and Hearn (2008) conclude their article by summarizing, "[w]hen students set goals that aid their improved understanding, and then identify criteria, self-evaluate their progress toward learning, reflect on their learning, and generate strategies for more learning, they will show improved performance with meaningful motivation."

The idea that student self-assessment has a valuable place in every classroom—coupled with the templates that encourage students to record their reflections and plans of action both before and after assessments—is the foundation for this guide. Using my experience in the classroom, I developed templates for **pre-assessment student-self reflections**, as well as **post-assessment student self-reflections**, in the hopes of helping students of nearly every age, teachers and parents alike better understand student learning through students' own self-reflection. *When referring to "post-assessment student self-reflections", I am referring to the process when the student reflects on his level of understanding after he has taken the assessment but before it has been evaluated (see* Figure 1.2*). Ideally, the student, teacher and parent would reflect a third time* **after** *the assessment has been evaluated on the student's work and determine if further action or intervention, reteaching or remediation, is needed. Moving on from a concept before the student has mastered it can be problematic in the long term.*

The Pre-Assessment Student Self-Reflection

I have used the pre-assessment student self-reflection many times in my own classroom to help students recognize what essential knowledge they have mastered, and with which concepts they are still struggling *before an assessment on the targeted material even occurs*. This is different from a pre-test or a study guide because the pre-assessment student self-reflection not only asks the student specifically about the different objectives; it also asks them to prove his/her ability in solving/explaining the objective, and to come up with a plan of action to fill in the gap if one exists. So, if the student determines that they are not able to explain the stated objective, the pre-assessment self-reflection requires them to identify a strategy to help gain better understanding.

Suggestions for intervention strategies may include the student asking for one-on-one assistance from a peer, teacher, parent or other trusted adult, reviewing notes, playing a game that enforces the material, using technology to gain better understanding and so on. These will look different at every grade level, content area and within each teacher's classroom. Equipped with this knowledge about their own understanding (or lack thereof), students can then determine what content they need to study, **and** how best to study it. Students determine and reflect on their own (mis)understanding of multiple key concepts **before** the test, exam or other assessment even occurs, and make an action plan to bridge the gap between where they are and where they need to be—before the assessment. I have found that the tone of the class is much less stressful when the student is given the chance to reflect on and realize his areas of weakness before the assessment and come up with

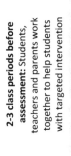

4-5 class periods before assessment: Students receive and complete pre-assessment student self-reflection, reflecting on their level of understanding and determine plans of action to fill in understanding gaps (Pre-Assessment Student Self-Reflection)

3-4 class periods before assessment: Teacher analyzes student reflections to determine individual or whole-class trends in misconceptions, and groups students according to needs for remediation or extension

2-3 class periods before assessment: Students, teachers and parents work together to help students with targeted intervention

Assessment day: Students take assessment and complete post-assessment reflection BEFORE TURNING IN ASSESSMENT for grade/evaluation (Post-Assessment Self-Reflection)

1-2 class periods after the post assessment: students, teachers and parents use assessment and Student reflections to analyze student performance and determine levels of true student understanding; further remediation is offered if necessary

Figure 1.2 Suggested general timeline of pre- and post-assessment student self-reflections.

A suggestion for students, teachers, and parents on how to time the student pre- and post-assessment student self-reflection based on the author's personal experience. The reflections, outcomes and timing will likely look different at each grade level and in each classroom.

Concept or Sample Question	DO YOU UNDERSTAND THIS CONCEPT?		
* Sample Question #1	YES ---------->	Explain:	
	NO, but I am going to do this to help my understanding	Review past assignments/ notes Draw picture	ask a friend or family member other: _____ _____
* Sample Question #2	YES ---------->	Explain:	
	NO, but I am going to do this to help my understanding	Play "fraction war" with a classmate, teacher or friend Use math app X to review	make flashcards other: _____ _____

Figure 1.3 Pre-assessment student self-reflection template.

A sample pre-assessment student self-reflection template. The desired outcomes are listed on the left column. Next to each one, the student is asked to reflect on her level of understanding **and** demonstrate mastery. If she cannot demonstrate mastery, she would choose an action plan from the ones given, or create her own, and follow through. Finally, after receiving additional instruction, she would circle back and demonstrate mastery. Note that the "action plans" will vary by subject, age, and ability of student.

a viable and effective plan of action. That way, there is ample time to build understanding, and no grade or evaluation has been tied to the level of student understanding at that point in time. Ideally, this process also gives the student's teacher and parent the opportunity to review the pre-assessment self-reflection with the student to either confirm understanding, or confirm and facilitate an effective strategy that will lead to student understanding.

One pre-assessment self-reflection template is shown in Figure 1.3 for better clarity. It is intended to be a template only and should be modified for student age, ability level and classroom norms. For example, an assessment filled with words may not appropriate for a 1st grader, who is perhaps better served by seeing a sample problem and then circling a picture of a check mark to indicate understanding or a question mark to indicate that the young student feels unsure of his/her ability. Other students and grade levels may need much more space on their papers than what is shown here to demonstrate mastery. It will look different in each class, and perhaps for each unit of study. Regarding specific classroom norms, it may be the case that a 5th grade teacher has approved certain math websites for students during this unit, in which case, offering a computer game would be a viable strategy listed under "No, but I am going to this to help my understanding." Other classes will, no doubt, have different rules about the use of technology. It is up to the individual teachers to inform students about the possible remediation strategies available to their students and amend this template accordingly.

In a lot of ways, the pre-assessment self-reflection functions as an interactive flow chart. The student is presented with a sample question, problem, or objective and then reflects on and determines his level of understanding of the concept. If he feels confident in his understanding, the "Yes" path takes him to a place for him to demonstrate his understanding. If he does not feel confident, the "No" path takes him to a place where several appropriate and relevant action items are suggested to help him gain mastery of the concept. (This step is critical in helping students determine effective study methods, as they so often stare blankly at an open textbook absorbing little or no content, and consider it studying.) The idea is that he will then circle back up to the "Yes" path once he has learned the content and can demonstrate his understanding. The process continues until the student can confidently answer "Yes" when asked if he understands a concept that will be assessed in the near future.

This model allows for the "growth mindset" in children. The students who reflect and can admit that they still have not mastered a concept should be far from feeling like they never will get there. This pre-assessment self-reflection is intended to help students see that they can choose strategies to help them learn and master the content. Without a plan in place to bridge the gap of where a student is and where she needs to be, it might be easy for the student to feel hopeless—like she never can and never will master the material. However, empowered to choose the best strategy for herself—based on preferred learning style, area of need, resources available, etc.,—the student can feel hopeful and confident that she has the tools, support, and ability needed to learn the content. Students are able to identify the goals, reflect on their ability to achieve the goal, and then come up with a plan to master any and all objectives that are still eluding them after initial instruction, but before any pressure or finality associated with assessment. With this framework, parents and teachers are also given the opportunity to intervene and offer remediation when the student is in an environment that is potentially much less stressful to the student.

Again, the sample pre-assessment self-reflection here is simply a suggested template and will need to be modified for student age and ability, as well as centered around strategies that are relevant to the students' particular classroom and environment.

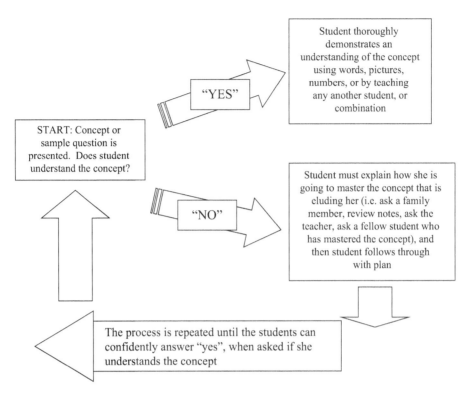

Figure 1.4 Asking the student about levels of understanding.

Students receive the pre-assessment self-reflections with the roughly five target concepts or sample problems listed down the left column. If a student answers, "Yes" to the question asking if he understands the concepts, he solidifies his answer by completing the "Explain" section. He can use words, pictures, expressions, equations, diagrams, excerpts from texts or notes, etc. to prove his full understanding. However, if the student reflects and realizes that he has not mastered the concept fully, his task changes. He must choose a strategy/plan from those listed, or write in his own preferred (but also approved) strategy, to learn the material. Once he has studied or sought out additional instruction, and feels that he has mastered the concept, he still must fill out the "Explain" section to fully demonstrate his understanding of the previously unknown material. He then turns in the pre-assessment self-reflection to the teacher. At that time, she has the opportunity to catch any misconceptions and/or offer extra assistance before the assessment even has been given. Ideally, parents are also able to review their child's self-reflection to confirm student understanding, and/or provide insights or raise concerns to the teacher and/or student himself.

While the individual templates will need to be class- and content-specific, the overarching concept and process is universal. First, begin by outlining the objectives and asking the student about their level of understanding for each one (Figure 1.4). If they respond, "Yes"—meaning they feel confident in their understanding—they must prove that they know the content (through words, expressions, equations, diagram, pictures, teaching the concept to another student, etc.). If they respond, "No"—meaning the student is unsure of their ability to demonstrate mastery—they must identify a strategy (presumably one taught and approved by the classroom teacher or parent), seek additional clarification and/or instruction, and then circle back to the part of the self-reflection where they can successfully demonstrate their understanding.

A key feature of the process is that the pre-assessment self-reflection is given to students four or five class meetings before the assessment is to take place. This allows students time to complete the self-reflection and for the teacher(s) (and if possible, parents) to analyze the results. This also allows for another essential part of the process: remediation and intervention *before the assessment even takes place*.

It is critical to note that the concepts listed down the left column of the pre-assessment self-reflection are not the exact items that will appear on the upcoming assessment. Rather, they are the objectives (or examples of the objectives) toward which the teachers have been leading the students throughout the unit. Good practice suggests that teachers, students, and parents know the goals and objectives the students are working toward before a unit even begins, so creating sample problems or lists of the concepts on the pre-assessment self-reflection is not giving anything away or unfairly giving an advantage to students. By no means is it cheating or enabling the students. Notice in the example of the fraction unit given here (Figure 1.5) that the first objective on the pre-assessment reflection asks "Which fraction of triangles is shaded?" The first three questions on the fraction assessment ask very similar (but not the same) questions ("What fraction of the rectangles below is shaded?," "Maria bought 12 eggs, but 1 was cracked. What fraction of the eggs was cracked?," and "What fraction of the rectangle is shaded?"). By completing the pre-assessment reflection question, the student has been given exposure to the type of question they can expect on the assessment, without getting the exact question that will be on the assessment.

Furthermore, because it is recommended that teachers set their sights on the goals before unit or individual lesson planning begins, the pre-assessment student reflection can easily be created before, or at the same time as, the assessment is created. The idea is that everyone—student, teacher, and parent—know the learning objectives before, during, and after instruction and assessment take place. The student is asked to monitor his own progress and level of understanding *before* the assessment so there is time for additional instruction before the assessment takes place.

In short, the student is notified of the learning objective and is instructed accordingly. Several days before the assessment, the student is asked to gauge and demonstrate his understanding. If he shows a lack of understanding, he is asked to come up with a strategy, relearn or review the material and then demonstrate understanding. It is during the days between the pre-assessment self-reflection and the actual assessment that the student fills in gaps or

Name _____ Date _____

Fraction Number Sense
Pre-Assessment Student Self-Reflection

Concept or Sample Question	DO YOU UNDERSTAND THIS CONCEPT?	
* Which fraction of triangles is shaded? △ ▲ △	YES ---------->	Explain:
	NO, but I am going to do this to help my understanding	Review past assignments/ notes ask a friend or family member Draw picture other: _____ _____

Name _____ Date _____

Fraction Number Sense

1. What fraction of the rectangles below is shaded?

Answer: _____

2. Maria bought 12 eggs, but 1 was cracked. What fraction of the eggs was cracked?

Answer: _____

3. What fraction of the rectangle is shaded?

Answer: _____

Figure 1.5 Pre-assessment student self-reflection example.

Note that the first objective of the pre-assessment student self-reflection aligns with the first three questions of the assessment, without being an exact copy of any of the questions. This allows the teacher, parent and, most importantly, the student to identify if the student has mastered the information that will be on the assessment without cheating or "teaching to the test".

clarifies misconceptions. If he can show mastery, he has shown he is prepared for the assessment and is perhaps ready for extensions. (In the unlikely event that every student demonstrates mastery in all set objectives, the teacher may choose to push up the date of the assessment and gain valuable instructional time for the next unit. No need to spend the three or four days between the pre-assessment self-reflection and the assessment reviewing material if everyone is ready for the assessment already.) Either way, the student is able to demonstrate understanding of the concept(s) before the assessment even takes place.

McMillan and Hearn (2008) state that:

> Reflection helps students think about what they know or have learned while they identify areas of confusion, so they can create new goals … [s]tudents benefit from explaining their work and their own evaluation of quality through reflective activities such as conferences, written correspondence with parents or peers, and written self-reflections or checklists.

The process I've outlined here simply gives students a chance to reflect, set goals, and remediate before an assessment takes place. However, the pre-assessment student self-reflection is a process that students will need to be taught and coached and will need to practice. Often times, I noticed that students rush through the pre-assessment paper, either mindlessly copying examples from class work to show their mastery or not following through with the strategy they chose to help them learn whatever material they are lacking. This defeats the point of the exercise.

One suggestion is to show students examples of two or three sample pre-assessment self-reflections like the ones shown in Figures 1.6 and 1.7. One is clearly insufficient and mostly unhelpful to the student, teachers, and parents. The other example is very valuable for showing what the student knows and what she still needs to work on.

Another strategy to try when introducing the pre-assessment student self-reflections is an exercise where you position your students as the "teachers." You set the scene as though they are in charge of teaching younger students a concept that they, the student-teachers know quite well—say adding $2 + 2$ if your students are in 3rd grade. You might show them two sample pre-assessment student self-reflections that have been filled out by the "younger students." One is quickly and thoughtlessly filled out and gives little insight into what the child was thinking when he incorrectly answered that $2 + 2 = 3$. Hopefully, your own students will see that without having information about what the sample student knows, it is hard to know how to help their

Concept or Sample Question	DO YOU UNDERSTAND THIS CONCEPT?		
* Round 84 to the nearest tens place. 3.NBT.A.1	YES ---------->	Explain: 84 ---> 80	
	NO, but I am going to do this to help my understanding	Review past assignments/ notes Draw picture	ask a friend or family member other: _____ _____
* Round 84 to the nearest hundreds place. 3.NBT.A.1	YES ---------->	Explain: 84 ---> 100	
	NO, but I am going to do this to help my understanding	Review past assignments/ notes Draw picture	ask a friend or family member other: _____ _____

Figure 1.6 Sample student pre-assessment self-reflection.

This example of the pre-assessment student self-reflection does not give the teacher or parent much information other than the student answered both questions correctly. This could mean that the student has a mastery of the material, but it could also be lucky guesses or that she got help (or answers) from a friend, or copied class notes without understanding. This would be a good example to show to students when teaching them about the self-reflections and the importance of students explaining and supporting their own thinking. It would be helpful to point out that the student did not support or prove her thinking and therefore, it does not help the teacher (and parents) get a real sense of what she knows or if she needs remediation or extra help.

students. You could then present the second sample student self-reflection. If your student-teachers can see that "the younger children" are drawing a correct picture of two objects and then another two objects, but then got an answer of 3, they may be able to put together that this sample student correctly drew two objects and another two objects, but then started counting at 0. How helpful to know that the sample child understands the concept of "putting together," and that the misunderstanding is with the fact that the sample child was starting at 0 rather than 1! You, as the teacher, would want to emphasize to your student-teachers that we cannot glean much information from Sample #1—other than the student needs some form of intervention— because that child did not let us know what he was thinking to get the answer of 3. Conversely, we know exactly what kind of intervention sample student #2 needs—practice with counting starting from 1.

Having your own students analyze the younger students' "easy" work can help solidify the value of them taking the time to do the pre-assessments themselves. By giving them a chance to see things from the "teacher's perspective" (Figures 1.8 and 1.9), you may help them to see how important it is to support their reflections with pictures, words, or whatever means they choose to demonstrate mastery.

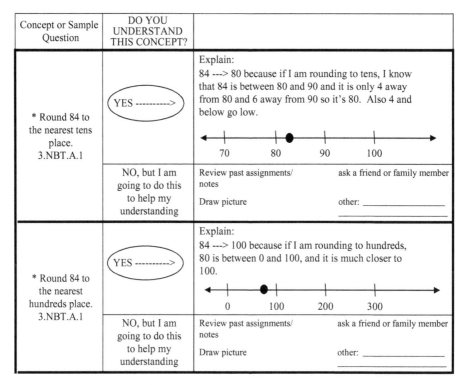

Concept or Sample Question	DO YOU UNDERSTAND THIS CONCEPT?	
* Round 84 to the nearest tens place. 3.NBT.A.1	YES --------->	Explain: 84 ---> 80 because if I am rounding to tens, I know that 84 is between 80 and 90 and it is only 4 away from 80 and 6 away from 90 so it's 80. Also 4 and below go low. (number line: 70 80 90 100, dot between 80 and 90)
	NO, but I am going to do this to help my understanding	Review past assignments/notes ask a friend or family member Draw picture other: _____
* Round 84 to the nearest hundreds place. 3.NBT.A.1	YES --------->	Explain: 84 ---> 100 because if I am rounding to hundreds, 80 is between 0 and 100, and it is much closer to 100. (number line: 0 100 200 300, dot between 0 and 100)
	NO, but I am going to do this to help my understanding	Review past assignments/notes ask a friend or family member Draw picture other: _____

Figure 1.7 Alternate student sample pre-assessment self-reflection.

Conversely, this example would be a helpful resource to show students when introducing self-reflections to demonstrate an ideal self-reflection. This student got the correct answers AND explained her thinking. The student, teacher and parents can feel confident that this student is has mastered the objectives. Her words, pictures and answers all indicate that she has an accurate understanding of rounding to the tens and hundreds place.

Concept or Sample Question	DO YOU UNDERSTAND THIS CONCEPT?	
* What is 2+2?	YES -----|---->	Explain: 3
	NO, but I am going to do this to help my understanding	Review past assignments/notes ask a friend or family member Draw picture other: _____

Figure 1.8 Positioning students as teachers.

This is a sample of what you might want to show your students when they are the "teachers" analyzing helpful and unhelpful self-reflections. This example is unhelpful because the student did not explain his thinking at all, so we cannot determine what caused the erroneous thinking.

Concept or Sample Question	DO YOU UNDERSTAND THIS CONCEPT?	
* What is 2+2?	YES ----)---->	Explain: ● ● ● ● 0 1 2 3
	NO, but I am going to do this to help my understanding	Review past assignments/ notes ask a friend or family member Draw picture other: _____ _____

Figures 1.9 Positioning students as teachers.

This example is very helpful because the student showed us that he know that 2 + 2 means "putting 2 and 2 together"; however, he is confused about which number to start counting from. This is helpful information that your students may uncover when given a chance to be the "teachers".

The Post-Assessment Student Self-Reflection

The post-assessment student self-reflections have also proved fantastically powerful in my own classroom. After completing each assessment (quiz, test, or other), but *before turning it in to the teacher for grading*, students are asked to rate each assessment item based on how they feel they did on each question. **At this point, students do not know if they answered the question correctly or not, so they are answering the post-assessment self-reflection based on how *they think* they did on each question.** The post-assessment student self-reflection can be the final page of an assessment, handed out when the assessment itself is given to the student. It can also be a quick question after each test item or a group of questions at the bottom of each test page, as shown here in Figure 1.10.

It does not need to be elaborate. Again, the student fills out the post-assessment self-reflection **before** his assessment is turned in or evaluated. Why? Because this post-assessment self-reflection asks the student to reflect

	Circle the choice that best describes how you felt about answering the questions 1-2.			
STOP	Question 1:	EASY	HARD, BUT I THINK I GOT IT	I GUESSED
	Question 2:	EASY	HARD, BUT I THINK I GOT IT	I GUESSED

Figure 1.10 Simplified post assessment self-reflection.

A simplified version of the post-assessment self-reflection that can be added after individual assessment items or after a group of items.

on how he *feels and thinks he did*, **without actually have confirmation that he got the questions right or wrong.**

In their article, Stallings and Tascoine (1996) describe a similar process that Stallings used with her high school students. After having students work independently on a quiz for 10 minutes, she allowed her students to describe, in writing, what they found easy on the quiz. The next part of the reflection was to determine which problems they were struggling with. From there, Stallings had the students group themselves in threes and finish the quiz. She explains of her student self-reflection process, "[w]riting down what they understood and what they did not understand helped them think more systematically about their processes of problem solving."

As is the case with the pre-assessment student self-reflection, the post-assessment student self-reflection formats vary based on age of students, questions asked and general design. The teacher uses the data to determine what areas need remediation, and what areas have been sufficiently mastered. Figure 1.11 is another example of one part of a basic post-assessment self-reflection that might be included with a unit math test. It might be stapled to the test as the last page or even handed out separately so the student can place the reflection next to each test question to be sure he remembers what each question was, what it was asking and how he answered it.

The value of the post-assessment student self-reflection may be best explained by analyzing two student samples. When we review the examples of post-assessment student self-reflections, we can begin to see the multiple facets of helpful insights about student understanding that we have captured.

Put a check next to each number that describes how you feel about it. Remember, this is only used to help you; please be honest.

Question Number	It is Very Easy	I Feel Pretty Good About This	I Could Use Some More Help	I Need A LOT More Help	I Have No Idea What the Question is Asking of Me
1.					
2.					
3.					
4.					
5.					
6.					
7.					
8.					
9.					
10.					

Figure 1.11 Post-assessment student self-reflection template.

One portion of one of the recommended post-assessment student self-reflection templates that asks students to review each question/item on the assessment and reflect on his level of understanding and perceived difficulty of it.

Put a check next to each number that describes how you feel about it. Remember, this is only used to help you; please be honest.					
Question Number	It is Very Easy	I Feel Pretty Good About This	I Could Use Some More Help	I Need A LOT More Help	I Have No Idea What the Question is Asking of Me
1	X				
2	X				
3.	x				
4.		X			
5.		X			
6.	X				
7.					X
8.				X	
9.					X
10.					x
STUDENT A's Post-Assessment Self-Reflection					

Put a check next to each number that describes how you feel about it. Remember, this is between you and me; be honest.					
Question Number	It is Very Easy	I Feel Pretty Good About This	I Could Use Some More Help	I Need A LOT More Help	I Have No Idea What the Question is Asking of Me
1	X				
2	X				
3.	X				
4.	X				
5.	X				
6.	X				
7.	X				
8.					X
9.					X
10.					X
STUDENT B's Post-Assessment Self-Reflection					

Figure 1.12 Samples from Students A and B.

A sample of (2) students' post-assessment self-reflections used for analysis by teachers. Each individual student's reflection uncovers that particular student's gauge of his level of understanding. A comparison of (2) or more student self-reflections done by the teacher can uncover whole-class trends of misunderstanding, faulty questions or poor teaching methodology.

In this case, the students were given the same 10-question math test (Figure 1.12). They were asked to complete the test and then, before turning in the test, they were asked to review each problem and "rate" how they feel they did on it. **Again, at this point, the students do not know if they answered the question correctly or not.** They have not yet turned in the test to the teacher for evaluation.

In this example, Student A seems to feel that she has a pretty good grasp on the concepts tested in problems 1–6; however, she needs more work on the concepts tested in problems 7–10. She answered "It is Very Easy" or "I Feel Pretty Good About This" for the first 6 problems; however for numbers 7–10, she answered that she either needs a lot more help or that she has no idea what the question is even asking.

The teacher would want to compare this self-reflection with Student A's test results. If she answered questions 1–6 correctly, both the student's reflection and the test results support the idea that Student A has mastered the concepts tests in questions 1–6. If Student A missed questions 1–6, or parts thereof, there is a disparity between what the student thinks she knows and what she demonstrated on the test. Certainly the wrong answers could be simple mistakes, so the teacher would want to have a brief conversation with Student A to determine the root of Student A's incorrect answer(s). Error analysis on Student A's answers or a quick chat might prove very helpful in determining if Student A made simple mistakes or if Student A has a deeper lack of understanding of those questions' concepts. If time allows, the teacher or parent of Student A may also ask why she felt "pretty good" about questions 4 and 5, rather than thinking they were "very easy." It's a small difference but may lead to the student sharing valuable insights about her understanding.

Similarly, if Student A missed questions 7–10, both the reflection and the test results suggest that Student A truly still does not understand the concepts at hand. If, however, Student A answered 7–10 correctly, there is strong evidence to suggest that A is a "lucky" guesser. **She admitted in the post-assessment self-reflection that she does not understand the concept, and yet got she answered the questions correctly; this is an especially helpful tool to determine who guessed luckily on multiple choice/answer tests.**

Now a quick look at Student B. Student B also recorded that she was confident in her understanding of 1–6. She answered "It is Very Easy" for all six questions. Unlike Student A, though, Student B feels secure in her understanding of problem 7. Again, the teacher would want to compare the test results with Student B's self-reflection to make sure everything she stated on her self-reflection was supported by her assessment results. Correct answers for questions 1–7 would support the idea that the student did master the material in those questions, and that she is aware that she has mastered that material. Student B also readily admitted that she does not understand questions 8–10. If she answered those questions correctly, she most likely guessed on them, or at least part of them. If she got them wrong, she is likely not surprised.

It is interesting to note that Student A and B had different feelings about question 7. Student A found it to be very difficult and Student B thought it was easy. Assuming Student A got it wrong and Student B got it right, the teacher can identify that Student A needs remediation, but the teacher's strategy for teaching, presenting, or reviewing the content in question 7 for Student B was effective for her. If many students answered question 7 correctly, the teacher can feel confident that the method of delivery was effective, and the students struggling with the concept are doing so because of the material and not the presentation of it.

What is arguably most powerful about these results, however, is the trend that *both* students struggled with the concepts tested in problems 8–10. The teacher would want to use these data to determine if this were a class-wide trend, or just an issue with these two particular students. Assuming most, or at least many, students had issues with questions 8–10, the teacher now has evidence she did not do a sufficient job presenting the information and must revisit the concepts with a new, fresh and more meaningful approach. There could also be a problem with the questions themselves, such as that they were poorly worded or unclear. If even a small group of the students readily admitted that they were struggling with the concepts in questions 8–10—**even if they answered the questions correctly**—the teacher needs to revisit the concept with the class. There is misunderstanding—either real or perceived—related to the concepts in those questions and the misunderstanding needs attention. Most likely, the students are not yet ready to move on from this concept.

Therefore, in addition to clearly showing how individual students feel about each assessment question, the post-assessment student self-reflections can also help teachers determine trends in their classroom that illuminate concepts that may not have been clearly taught or understood. It is easier for teachers to blame students for their lack of understanding, than reflect on the effectiveness of their own delivery. However, if a group of students all miss one question or type of question, there is good reason to believe that the teacher's method of explanation was not effective or that the question was faulty. By comparing the students' post-assessment self-reflections, and determining trends, teachers can help pinpoint which concepts may need to be revisited and re-taught because the initial methodology was not effective, and therefore, a different approach need to be taken.

Additionally, this post-assessment self-reflection also eliminates the problem of "lucky guessing," especially on multiple choice test questions. On the post-assessment self-reflection, if a student marks the choice, "I Have No Idea What This Question is Asking of Me" for a specific question, but still managed to guess the correct answer, the teacher will not mistakenly assume that the student understands the content. This could be the case with Student A on questions 7, 9, and 10 if she had answered those test questions correctly, but admitted that she "had no idea what [these] question[s] were asking of [her]." So often students can fly under the radar with lucky guessing; however the post-assessment self-reflection can be a wonderful resource at helping to determine a single student or group of students' level of understanding.

Other very valuable information can be gleaned from other questions posed to students in the post-assessment student-reflections, based on the questions each teacher chooses to incorporate in the self-reflections. For example, on this template (Figure 1.13), there are two questions that ask students about the "easiest" and "most challenging" aspects of the assessment. They can potentially give teachers broad ideas of their students' understanding.

If many students answer that questions 4, 5, and 6 were "easiest" and they did answer those questions correctly, the teacher can feel confident that her methods of teaching the concepts related to those questions were effective,

What part of the test did you think was easiest?

_____

_____

_____

What part of the test was most challenging for you?

_____

_____

_____

Figure 1.13 Easiest and most challenging parts.

An optional addition to the post-assessment student self-reflection that asks students about what they perceive to be the "easiest" and the "hardest" parts or questions of the assessment. This can be helpful in identifying too heavy of a reliance on "tricks" or mnemonics if, for example, the students concludes that parts of the test were "easy", but then failed to answer them quickly. The "challenging" question can help students and teachers see that the students are capable of mastering difficult materials.

and that the students did master the concepts. If many students answer that 4–6 were "easiest," but do not have the correct answers to back up those claims, the teacher needs to look again to see what is giving her students this false self-confidence. Often times, especially in math, too many "tricks" that students easily confuse are the culprit. The students rely so heavily on tricks, or even algorithms, without fully understanding the value of the numbers and therefore lack the number sense and understanding to find mistakes or recognize gross errors. They find these questions "easy" because they have tricks to solve them, but if the trick is misremembered or not perfectly executed, students cannot see the error of their ways or recognize that their answers are not reasonable.

Similarly, if most students mark that 7–9 are "most challenging" and have incorrect answers to back up their claim of difficulty, the teacher may need to reevaluate her teaching strategies. Ideally, students would say that 7–9 are "most challenging," but still answer the question correctly. We, as educators, want to make sure our students feel like they are accomplishing great feats with great success; it keeps them engaged. It's my experience that students who recognize that a problem or concept is challenging, and yet still "solvable," tend to gain confidence in their abilities. It is good for students to admit that the questions make them think.

Additionally, in select post-assessment self-reflections, teachers can use the final question (or similar version thereof), "Which problems, if any, did you correct while checking over your work?," to emphasize the importance and value of students reviewing their work before turning it in to be evaluated (Figure 1.14).

You should have checked your work before turning it in. Please tell me which problems, if any, you were able to correct because you checked your work.

_____

_____

Figure 1.14 Students are asked to review their work before it is evaluated.

Another optional question that may be appropriate for a post-assessment self-reflection when the teacher is hoping to emphasize the value of checking over one's work before turning it in for evaluation. See Vignette 3 in Chapter 6 for a sample conversation between student and teacher.

It is so powerful for the student to see that, for example, his score may have been a "C" had he not checked over his work, but that because he took the time to do so, he caught two mistakes and raised his grade to a "B," for example. A very brief conversation between teacher and student (where the value of checking work before turning in a test is discussed) can be the proof students need to change their attitudes (and general disdain) about the value of proofreading and checking work.

In addition to being extremely useful tools for teachers and students, parents can use both the pre- and post-assessment student self-reflections to take active roles in their child's learning. By reviewing their child's responses to the pre-assessment reflection, parents can gather a sense of what materials will be tested, and with which of those concepts in particular their child needs help *before the assessment even takes place*. Furthermore, close analysis of their child's post-assessment self-reflection can help parents understand what concepts are still eluding their child even after the assessment, and can be wonderfully helpful in determining areas needing continued intervention. See the chapter titled, "From the Parent's Perspective" for an example of how parents can be another significant part of this sequence. This will look very different in each household, of course. Many parents do not have the time or flexibility in their schedule to look over their child's pre- and post-assessment self-reflections. Many parents believe that they themselves are "bad" at the subject and should not be helping their child with anything related to it. Sometimes there are language barriers, or other hurdles that need to be addressed. Whatever the reason, parents should feel that any time and effort that they can give to their child is helpful. If the parent simply asks the child about his self-reflections and earnestly listens to the child's responses, there is value. If the parent can watch a subject-specific video from the internet with the child, there is value. If the parent can ask a friend or neighbor for a bit of related information, there is value. Having a parent show sincere interest in their child's academic journey—in whatever form or fashion that looks like—is so valuable.

Therefore, the pre- and post-assessment self-reflections enable and encourage students to take responsibility for their own learning. They also allow the teacher to collect data on each individual student for each different assessment, as well as class trends to determine the causes of misconstrued or ill-understood concepts. Finally, parents can take a more proactive role in their child's learning by understanding what concepts their child is working on in school, and whether or not remediation is needed, both before and after assessments have been given.

A QUICK NOTE ABOUT THE VALUE SELF-REFLECTIONS IN ALL CLASSROOMS

For consistency and maximum clarity, the example self-assessments shown in these first chapters are mainly in math-centered; however, these pre- and post-assessment self-reflections can and should be adapted for language arts, social studies, science, the arts, and so on. Examples of sample self-assessments in a couple of subject areas, other than math, follow in subsequent chapters. It would be impossible to show examples for each discipline, but here are few examples of how the pre- and post- student self-reflections might be helpful in other areas of study. For example, music teachers may customize these pre- and post-assessment student self-reflections to ask about mastering songs on the recorder or learning the notes on string instruments. Valle, et al. (2016) explain:

> In music, self-assessment is a key element of effective independent practice (McPherson, et al). During self-assessment, students critique their work according to explicitly stated expectations, usually in the form of goals or criteria, and then engage in a revision process to improve their work. Self-assessment serves the purpose of improving the quality of first attempts at a piece of work so that the finished product or performance meets or exceeds expectations…

Middle school science teachers may ask students to reflect on their proficiency in drawing, labeling, and explaining the parts of an atom. A government teacher may ask students to reflect on their knowledge of the three branches of government before an assessment takes place. Likewise, there is significant evidence to support the idea that college students and pre-service professionals gain much by incorporating self-assessment into their repertoire of learning strategies. Donald Woods (1987) posits that:

> We can realistically judge our own performance and effectively monitor our own learning. This still is required in order to continue

learning after graduation or for professionals to continually assess
their own work. Students need to become critical appraisers of their
own work and to acquire a sophisticated appreciation of the standards in their disciplines."

In that same vein, teachers themselves can and should use these reflections
to become better educators.

It is my belief that all students can benefit from being asked to take the
time to reflect on their strengths and weaknesses, progress and misconceptions. Teachers and parents also stand to learn valuable information that has
the potential to maximize students' learning.

2

Setting the Scene

In her article, McDonald (2007) states that "[s]elf assessment is an integral part of both portfolio and authentic assessment. It involves reflecting on past achievements, critically evaluating present performance, and planning future goals." She makes it clear, however, that most children do not start their educational careers already knowing how to self-assess. To that point, teachers (and perhaps parents as well) should receive formal or informal training on how to facilitate student self-assessment. McDonald (2007) explains that:

> Self assessment may be viewed as the act of evaluating or monitoring one's own level of knowledge, performance, and understanding in a metacognitive framework, taking into account the contexts in which it occurs. Self assessment involves the individual making an informed assessment of his or her own work, with an appreciation for and the understanding of those concepts of quality upheld and practiced by the adjudicators of his or her work. Clearly, the honing of self-assessment skills would not naturally be endowed upon an individual but requires formal training. It also requires formal training on the part of the teachers so that they may effectively integrate into classroom teaching and learning.

DOI: 10.4324/9781003329176-2

So what does this look like inside a classroom?

In my experience, the most important factor in effective student self-assessment is a safe and trust-filled classroom environment. Students must feel comfortable not only examining their work—looking for strengths and weaknesses—but also then sharing them with trusted adults—teachers and ideally parents or caregivers. A "safe and trust-filled classroom" will look different for every teacher and every grade level. I would posit that the most important aspect is that teachers set the tone and expectation that mistakes are never things to be embarrassed by, but rather rich opportunities from which the student and his peers can learn. Unfortunately, it seems that younger children learn very quickly that a mistake or lack of understanding is something to hide. It is our job as educators and parents to make it abundantly clear that it is through reflection, asking clarifying questions and admitting uncertainty that we, as lifelong learners, continue to grow and master new skills.

As mentioned in the previous chapter, showing your students (and even their parents) examples of "helpful" and "unhelpful" student self-reflections can be very beneficial in getting students (and parents) to recognize the worth of these self-reflections. Another suggestion when introducing the idea of self-assessment to students might include asking students to perform or complete a task that is unlike most of what students see in that particular class. For example, a 4th grade general education teacher might tell her students that their objective for the class is to create a picture or schematic diagram of an invention that solves a problem in the world. This particular project idea is very open-ended and, in fact, may be perceived as fun by some or all of the students. The teacher might provide a list of requirements for the invention, such as ones listed here:

◆ your invention must be able to be made with household items
◆ your picture/diagram must be labeled and the invention named
◆ your invention must solve a problem in the world and that problem must be written on the paper
◆ your invention must something that could be replicated by others

The teacher would present the project and carefully review the project objectives, modeling and answering questions as they arise or are needed.

Students would then be asked to fill out a quick "pre-assignment reflection" like Figure 2.1.

By doing this pre-assessment self-reflection, students are getting used to the process of recognizing the objectives of the assessment, reflecting on their ability and then determining if any intervention or additional outside help is needed—all in a low-stakes, low-pressure environment.

Concept or Sample Question	DO YOU UNDERSTAND THIS CONCEPT?	
* I can create an invention that is made of household items.	YES --------->	Explain:
	NO, but I am going to do this to help my understanding	Spend time brainstorming ideas ask a friend for more information about what this means Ask my teacher for help other: _____ _____
* I can label my picture and name my invention	YES --------->	Explain:
	NO, but I am going to do this to help my understanding	Draw first and then see what names seem best ask a friend or family member for help with spelling Ask my teacher what labeling means other: _____ _____
* I can create an invention that solves a problem	YES --------->	Explain:
	NO, but I am going to do this to help my understanding	List problems first and then come up with inventionideas ask a friend for more information or suggestions Ask my teacher for help other: _____ _____
* I can create a machine that can be easily replicated	YES --------->	Explain:
	NO, but I am going to do this to help my understanding	Draw an invention and then make changes so it can be copied ask a friend or family member for help or ideas Ask my teacher for help other: _____ _____

Figure 2.1 Pre-assignment reflection.

In this example, the teacher created an "off-topic" project and related pre-assessment self-reflection so her students could focus on the bigger process rather than get overwhelmed by the idea of learning new material **and** having to reflect on their own understanding, creating and implementing plans of action and then reflecting on progress once again.

Then, the students are given time to complete the project. Before they turn in or present the final design/picture, they would be asked to fill out a "post-assessment self-reflection" like this one (Figure 2.2).

Again, this assignment is intentionally "off-subject" and somewhat whimsical so that the students can focus on the process of goal-setting, creating action plans and self-reflection. Before the students turn in their inventions, I would suggest that they be given time to share their inventions and self-reflections with a single peer or small group of peers. The teacher should

	Yes	I don't know	Thoughts/Questions?
I designed an invention that is made of household items.			
I labeled my invention and gave it a name.			
My invention solves a problem.			
My invention could be made others easily.			

Figure 2.2 Post-assessment self-reflection.

The post-assessment student self-reflection that may be associated with the "fun" project mentioned in the task. Introducing the idea of pre- and post-assessment self-reflections to students using projects that are more capricious can help students practice the skill of self-reflection without the stress of worrying about new, content-heavy information.

model what an honest and constructive conversation might look like within a group of peers. For instance,

> Kayla, I think your Invention X is a great idea. I like how you made it out of household items like plastic straws and foil. I see the title on the top of the page, but I don't see any labels yet. One of the objectives was to add labels to the invention and you marked that you did add a label. Do you know what a label is? Diseha, could you show Kayla how you labeled your invention here and here? Kayla, are there any other parts of the assignment that were confusing or unclear?

While this "invention" project may not resonate with older students, the idea that there is a lot of benefit in introducing the practice of student self-reflection first with "fun" topics holds water at all ages and grade levels. Teachers should adapt the above example to best fit their students' abilities and ages. Some examples of "objectives" that might work well with students of all ages when introducing them to and coaching them on self-reflections may be:

◆ watching a familiar movie and finding specific parts that show X objectives;
◆ choosing your favorite book or piece of writing and finding specific parts that show X objectives;
◆ writing a letter, poem, song to a friend or relative that explain X objectives;
◆ drawing a picture that explains or shows X;
◆ going for a walk outside and looking for examples of X;

◆ listening to a song to hear X;
◆ examining a photograph to find X.

Practicing reflection and self-assessment in this type of a low-stakes environment may help students so much. It gives them a chance to reflect, ask questions, share their insights with peers and, ideally, gain confidence in taking responsibility for their own learning and achievement. This whole process might need to be repeated several times before the teacher asks students to implement the process on more academic content. A scaffolded approach like this one that allows students to start practicing reflection and planning first with a light activity may help make the process less daunting. With practice and coaching, students should become comfortable reflecting on their ability in relation to the set academic objectives, determining a plan for success where necessary, and then reflecting on their strengths and weaknesses.

Getting Students to Use the Pre- and Post-Assessment Self-Reflections

The age and ability of the student are significant considerations in her ability to use the pre- and post-assessment self-reflections in a worthwhile fashion. It's been my experience that younger children tend to be more open and willing to share misconceptions; however, they often lack the writing skills and vocabulary needed to accurately convey their thinking. Older students, on the other hand, often have become more self-conscious—fearful of ridicule from peers, parents and perhaps, even teachers—and may require a little more practice and assurance that their results will be kept confidential.

ELECTRONIC OR PAPER?

If the pre- and post-assessment self-reflections seems like a bunch of extra paper, and your preferred medium for assignments and assessments is the computer or tablet, by all means, present the self-reflections in those formats. There is no reason a student cannot answer these questions electronically. There is no reason you can't analyze and organize the data electronically. In fact, those teachers who are spreadsheet-savvy may prefer to do it electronically. Once created, the templates are very easy to change and modify for each specific assessment and learning goal.

One thing to consider is how you will get the information to the parents (and/or back to the students), if there is a need for them to review it. If you have a system of communicating with parents electronically, it should not be an issue. The problem arises when there are families who do not have reliable access to the internet and electronic messages and files, or if there are privacy issues with protecting student work. Perhaps in these instances, it would make the most sense to print out the self-reflections and send paper copies home with students.

The best-case scenario is when a student feel comfortable enough to be completely honest with themself, their parents/caregivers and their teacher(s) about their level of understanding. Teachers and parents must stress the value of metacognition and must demonstrate and model it repeatedly. It is important to note that the reflections that teachers and parents get from students at the beginning of each school year might be less valuable than the ones received at the end of the year. Students must feel comfortable and at ease—ready and willing to take risks—and usually, this is not established in the first couple of days or weeks of school. Coaching and encouraging students to continue to try to identify their weaknesses (and strengths!) is an arduous, but worthwhile process. Bercher (2012) states that "[o]ften students cannot accurately monitor their progress toward learning goals and overestimate mastery of content, leading to overconfidence and, subsequently, poor academic performance." With repeated practice and opportunities to see the value of self-reflections, students of all ages should become better at accurately assessing themselves. Having a teacher demonstrate the process in an authentic setting by choosing a concept that is unfamiliar to the teacher herself may help show the students that reflection and action planning is helpful, rather than embarrassing.

Younger children will likely require relatively simplistic pre- and post-assessment self-reflections, as compared to older peers. Even students who have not mastered reading or have limited writing abilities can use the self-reflections if they are read aloud, or accompanied by pictures and examples of the concepts at hand. Rather than asking young children to write detailed sentences about their level of understanding, simple boxes to check or emojis to circle, for example, can get the job done.

HOW DO I MAKE THE PRE- AND POST-ASSESSMENT SELF-REFLECTION PART OF MY CLASSROOM ENVIRONMENT?

As with any new initiative introduced to your students, the self-reflections must be modeled and repeated by you to your students. If it is possible to start at the beginning of the year, I highly recommend that the self-reflections become a natural part of all assessments from Day 1 until the last assessment is given each year. Ideally, you will be able to incorporate a pattern of pre-assessment self-reflection, assessment, post-assessment self-reflection, repeat. Students should learn to expect the self-reflections, and, perhaps, even look forward to them. They should want to express their level of understanding, either by demonstrating mastery or by admitting that they need help to an audience that has compassionate **and** proactive ears.

I suggest showing your students several of past students' self-reflections (keeping privacy in mind, of course), showing them exemplars from this guide, or making up examples on your own. Your students need to see for themselves (and be reminded of often) the value in being honest about what they know with you, their parents and themselves. For some students, this is easy. They will readily ask for help or admit confusion, even without the self-reflection. If possible, ask those students to partner up with the more reticent ones, if they are willing to—and share how it can be intimidating at first to admit that they need help, but then how great it feels to get much-needed help, and then succeed. For other students, this will be a challenge that requires constant and consistent attention. Try sharing personal stories about when you had to admit that you didn't know something and how by being honest about your need for further instruction, you were able to come up with a plan of action to better your position.

Another very important consideration is equity. Are the students who have special needs or learning differences getting accommodations that make self-assessment manageable for them? In her article, Hill (1995) points out that "[s]elf assessment also needs to be fair. Herman (1992) warns that performance assessments (including self assessment) are as likely to disadvantage minority students from different racial, cultural and socio-economic groups as traditional measures." While, Hill and Herman's research is older, it is still relevant. Johansson (2013) supports these ideas further by citing:

Kuncel et al. (2005) also discussed socioeconomic status (SES) differences in students' self assessments after having found that the self-reported grades and actual grades of minority groups of students were lower than those of nonminority students. In the study by Kuncel and his colleagues, the minority groups typically came from the lower SES backgrounds. Although the research community has not widely studied the influence of SES on students' self-assessments, it seems possible that SES may relate to the ability to make accurate such assessments.

In these cases, I would encourage general education teachers to collaborate with the specialists to make similar modifications and accommodations to the pre- and post-assessment reflections that they make for the class assignments and assessments. For instance, will the child have a better chance at success if she can orally demonstrate mastery, rather than writing down a skill? Will a child process the reflection objectives better if they are read aloud to him, or if he is able to point to a picture, rather than having to read or say the answer? Is a particular child better suited to answer 2–3 objectives rather than 4–5? If a child's home environment is not conducive to homework, perhaps allowing the student to complete the reflections during the school day is a more equitable solution. Whatever accommodation is typically used to level the playing field for your special needs students also should be used in the self-reflections, whenever possible.

Hill continues in her article (1995) that "there are times when self assessment is not beneficial ... This might be the case when students are very hard on themselves or don't know the criteria by which to judge their learning." In these instances, I believe it would be beneficial to take a step back and remind students of the reason for the reflections at all. Continuing to let them practice thinking metacognitively in high- and low-stakes environments may help reluctant or overly self-critical students immensely. In Bercher's (2012) article, she reiterates the conclusion that "[a]ccurate self-assessment of one's knowledge and performance leads to more effective use of feedback, improved time management and appropriate goal setting (Hacker et al., 2000)."

Another topic requiring attention centers around students who overstate their abilities in a pre-assessment setting. Bercher (2012) explains:

> [i]n the study of predictive and postdictive judgments of students by Hacker et al. (2000), exaggerated predictive test performance was demonstrated by lower-performing students. These students exhibited very poor self-assessment and self-evaluation of their knowledge, which negatively impacted their academic future. They not only lacked knowledge of course content, but also-and more seriously-lacked an awareness of their own knowledge deficits. Often these students presented unrealistic and overly optimistic judgments of their performance even when faced with evidence of low performance.

Ehrlinger, Johnson, Banner, Dunning, & Kruger (2008) extrapolated from Blackwell et al. and their own research that when students believe that their level of intelligence is not fixed, they may be able to more accurately self-assess. They state:

School children who are taught that intelligence is malleable get more excited about learning, become more motivated in the classroom and achieve better grades (Blackwell, Trzesniewski, & Dweck, 2007). Thus, teaching individuals that intelligence is malleable might lead to more accurate self-assessments because this measure leads to an improvement of knowledge and skill that, in and of itself, promotes greater self-insight.

It is so important for students to reflect on their abilities as accurately as possible, as what they conclude about their ability level often dictates their subsequent actions. Oscarson (2009) focuses on self-assessment of language, but I believe it applies to all areas of learning. She explains:

> students' over- or underestimations of their knowledge [is important if it will] lead them to make the wrong assumptions about their learning needs. Students who overestimate their language proficiency may believe that they are in control of things they really do not grasp, and thus do not take in skills that they in reality need to learn. Students who underestimate their competence may possibly apply themselves to work on areas they actually already master and, in doing so, fail to challenge themselves. The making of reliable and realistic self-assessments is therefore an important part of the student being able to focus correctly, and learn efficiently.

To avoid students overestimating or underestimating their abilities and conceptual understanding, they need to be given repeated opportunities to reflect, with the comfort of mind knowing that their responses will not be used for any other purpose than to help them. Additionally, teachers and parents should also emphasize the belief that students' intelligence and abilities can be developed with hard work and a growth mindset. Students of all ages, abilities and backgrounds must practice reflecting both before and after assessments, and feel comfortable sharing the results of their reflections with trusted adults.

3
From the Student's Perspective

We begin with a look at how students are intended to use the pre- and post-assessment self-reflections, as their growth, understanding and success is the focus of all three parties' (student, teacher and parents') attention. Imagine for the sake of better understanding, the perspective of "Ryan", a 5th grade student who has been studying fraction number sense for the past two weeks in his math class. Ryan typically struggles with math, but usually flies under the radar because he tends to stay quiet in class and get help with his homework from a parent, who means well, but perhaps does too much of the work for him. Given these factors, it is quite possible Ryan might slip through the cracks in most classrooms because he is so good at blending in, nodding his head in agreement and repeating what other students have said in class before him.

My teacher has announced that there will be an exam on Friday, and today is Monday. I muddled my way through the past two weeks, and I am not sure I know exactly what is going on, but I have been able to get help with my homework from my mom, stay fairly quiet in class and feel that I have not attracted much attention to myself. Of course, I've been here before. This strategy works fine most days … until test time comes, and sure enough, that test on Friday is staring me in the face.

However, for homework tonight, rather than worksheets or textbook problems, my math teacher gives me the Pre-Assessment Self-Reflection. We've done these before and it's nice to know what is going to be on the test.

DOI: 10.4324/9781003329176-3

I know I'm really good at some of the stuff, but not at everything, and I know my teacher, friend and Mom will help me with the stuff I don't get. Everybody keeps saying that I just have to let them know. I don't like raising my hand in class when I have a question because I don't want everyone to look at me; usually, I don't say anything. I've started writing more notes about what confuses me to my Mom and my teacher on the self-reflections because that's easier than asking for help in class.

So, I take the pre-assessment self-reflection home and begin reading through it. The first question down the left column asks me if I can identify which fraction is shaded. That's easy because I know I just have to count the ones that are gray and put that number on the top and the rest of the ones are on the bottom (*see the incorrect answer that Ryan writes in his reflection*).

Next, I have to find three equivalent fractions for 2/3. No problem. That is one that we have talked about a lot in school and plus, my friend showed me that you can put 0's after the numbers in the top and bottom and it is always equivalent. I have also memorized 1 other fraction that is equivalent to 2/3:4/6, 20/30, 200/300 and 2,000/3,000. I circle the "yes" in the middle column of the assessment and in the column on the right where it says "Explain", I list the equivalent fractions that I have memorized.

The third question of the pre-assessment asks me to compare two fractions, specifically 1/3 and 3/4. This is where things get a little harder for me. Both fractions are familiar to me, however I consistently forget the trick where you have to cross multiply one numerator with one denominator and then zigzag up or down, or maybe I have to add (or is it multiply?) each fraction by 0 or 1 or something like that. Rather than try to make something up, I have the option here to circle, "No, I don't know" and come up with a plan of action. Who can I ask? I know that this is probably the best time to admit that I need help, since that it is still four days before the test, so there isn't a lot of pressure. I was a little scared to admit what I was struggling to understand the first couple times we did these reflections because I didn't think my Mom or the teacher would want to know that I don't really get the stuff we're tested on, but each time they give me a "high five", say they're proud of me for admitting what I don't know yet, and then they both try to help me get better—all before the test even happens! So I tell my teacher that I am going to ask my Mom for help on this one.

The fourth question asks me to order fractions. I don't really know how to do this and I don't think my Mom does either, so I'm just going to tell my teacher that I really need help from her.

[Later that evening after Ryan and his mom have talked about fractions] My Mom reminded me about the trick where I multiply the top number of the first fraction with the bottom number of the second, and zigzag back—and then do that again with the second fraction. I know that 9 is bigger than 4, so 3/4 is bigger than1/3 (Figure 3.1).

A side note: In this example, this student is comfortable realizing, and then admitting his misunderstandings and misconceptions to his teacher, parent or friend. While this is an entirely possible scenario, it can only be accomplished in a classroom environment that is safe. Establishing that safe environment certainly takes time and effort on the part of the teachers, students and parents, but it is critical to the success of the student self-reflections. Teachers modeling and sharing their own mistakes, and reassuring students that mistakes are learning opportunities may help set the right tone. Teachers may even want to demonstrate this process with content that is slightly "over their heads" as well, showing students that they, too, need to reflect, make plans for filling in gaps of knowledge and keep a growth mindset at all times.

It is Tuesday morning in math class and my teacher collects our pre-assessment self-reflections. Math class goes on as it has for the past two weeks and I have found that if I just sit quietly and act like I know what is going on, usually no one calls on me.

Now, Wednesday has arrived and my teacher hands each one of my classmates and me a note card as we walk into the door. Mine says "3" and I notice that my friend, Ben, who is a math whiz, gets a card that has a "2," while Carmen, my other good friend, gets a "4." Our teacher explains that each group is going to work at different stations today and explains where we are each to go. She's always making little grids with our groups and times to tell us where to go for each station.

Ben goes to the independent work station to start, while both Carmen and I are with our teacher to start. It is at this first station that our teacher pulls out the self-assessments that we turned in on Monday and has us look at the first problem. We use pictures of all different types of fractions to figure out the name of each one. We also use manipulatives to work through the second problem. Our teacher even lets us explore other fractions with a similar-sized paper candy bar. We use fraction bars, fraction circles and even play some games with fractions. At first, I felt a little embarrassed that I had this answer wrong, but it turns out that a lot of my classmates also had a hard time. For the 2nd station, I work with Mr. X, who comes in to help during math time, and we do more practice with fraction circles. Carmen is working

Name **Ryan**   Date_____

Fraction Number Sense
Pre-Assessment Student Self-Reflection

Concept or Sample Question	DO YOU UNDERSTAND THIS CONCEPT?	
* Which fraction of triangles is shaded? △ ▲ △	YES --------->	Explain: $\frac{1}{2}$ because 1 is dark and 2 are white
	NO, but I am going to do this to help my understanding	Review past assignments/notes ask a friend or family member Draw picture other: _____ _____
* List 3 equivalent fractions to $\frac{2}{3}$	YES --------->	Explain: $\frac{20}{30}$, $\frac{200}{300}$, $\frac{2,000}{3,000}$ $\frac{4}{6}$
	NO, but I am going to do this to help my understanding	Review past assignments/notes ask a friend or family member Draw picture other: _____ _____

* Compare using <, > or =
 	
$\frac{1}{3}$ — $\frac{3}{4}$
	YES --------->	Explain:
		
		$\frac{1}{3}$ ✗ $\frac{3}{4}$ 9 is bigger
		  4 9 than 4 so $\frac{3}{4}$
		                    is bigger than $\frac{1}{3}$

	NO, but I am going to do this to help my understanding	Review past assignments/notes ask a friend or family member Draw picture other: _____ my mom _____ now I know
* Order these fractions from LEAST to GREATEST: $\frac{1}{2}$, $\frac{2}{8}$, $\frac{1}{10}$	YES --------->	Explain: ???????
	NO, but I am going to do this to help my understanding	Review past assignments/notes ask a friend or family member Draw picture other: I need help from you

Figure 3.1 Ryan's pre-assessment self-reflection.

on the computer for this station and Ben is in a small group with three other students. For the final station, we are back in one large whole-class group.

On Thursday, my teacher pulls Carmen and me in a small group and asks us a bunch of questions about equivalent fractions. I even get to work with Mr. X again, and then the rest of the time, I get to work with my friends. For the past two nights, my Mom and I have been playing fraction games at home that my teacher sent home. We had to cut out the cards with the fractions on them, but we use them every night for a bunch of different games. They're fun, especially because I usually win!

Friday is here and so is the test. I feel pretty good about most stuff on it. Before we can turn in the test, my teacher has us fill out the post-assessment self-reflection. I go back through each question on the test quickly to remind me how I felt about it, as I put checks on the reflection. I admit that while I feel really good about questions 1–6 (identifying fractions and finding equivalent fractions), and I think I did OK on 7–9 (comparing fractions), but I still had some trouble on numbers 10–12 (ordering fractions).

My teacher also always makes us tell her which questions we changed our answers for, and for me, it was number 6. When trying to find an equivalent fraction to 4/5, I first put 6/7 as the answer. Then when I checked my work, I figured out that the answer should be 8/10. I added 2/2 to 4/5's numerator and denominator instead of multiplying by 2/2, which I know is really 1. Plus, I just knew that 6/7 is not equivalent to 4/5.

Now, it's Monday and we get our tests back. I know that my teacher will have us look at our tests and go into more small groups. I got an 8/12 which is OK. I wanted to get all of the questions right, but I knew that #10, #11 and #12 were going to be wrong. I see that I messed up the comparing fractions ones, too (#8). I did the zigzags right, I think, but I wrote the problem backwards and didn't flip the sign. I am sure that in my group in math today we will be talking about ordering fractions since that is something I still need to work on. I'll take my test home to my Mom so she can look at it and ask me a bunch of questions. She always does this after tests, and I'm sure she'll ask me to explain to her how to do different questions on this test. We'll probably play more fraction games, which is actually pretty fun!

4

From the Teacher's Perspective

Establishing a Safe Environment Where Students Will Take Risks and Be Honest with Themselves, Their Parent(s) and You

The pre- and post-assessment student self-reflections are more or less meaningless if students do not feel comfortable sharing their strengths and weaknesses with their teacher (and parents). It is absolutely essential for teachers to establish a rapport with their students that allows them to feel at ease admitting what they don't know both before and after assessments. Teachers are tasked with explaining the fact that their pre- and post-assessment self-reflections and assessment results will be kept confidential. I always include a written and verbal reminder when asking students to fill out the reflections. Something simple like, "Remember this reflection is just between you and me. Please be honest" seems sufficient. At parent–teacher conferences, I also explain the purpose of the student self-reflections and urge parents to use the information students share only in positive ways.

If entire schools and, ideally, entire districts adopt the practice of pre- and post-assessment student self-reflections, the work of the teacher and parent is significantly reduced. I've found that younger students are usually willing and, often times, *eager* to share their strengths and weaknesses. It is only after a negative self-awareness develops that students begin to second guess the

DOI: 10.4324/9781003329176-4

value of sharing their misunderstandings for fear of being ridiculed by peers, teachers or parents.

Teachers must set up a classroom experience where students learn from one another's right, as well as wrong, answers. Having students share their thinking aloud from the very start is a great way to encourage a positive and safe classroom environment. This type of teaching methodology encourages students to freely share their thinking. Because successes *as well as mistakes* are used as teaching points, there is no shame with public errors or misunderstandings.

SUGGESTIONS FOR TEACHERS

◆ Explain the theory behind student self-reflections during Back-to-School nights, parent–teacher conferences and newsletters

◆ With the consent of administration, implement self-reflections at a school-wide level; if parents and students learn about self-reflections at an early age and realize it is a school-wide procedure, there is no need to introduce the concept year after year

◆ Host Family Math/Science/Reading Nights in which parents and students work together to solve problems and discuss different strategies among themselves, other students and their families, and the teacher (s)

◆ Remind parents often that you are there to answer questions and provide additional resources for their children by emailing and calling often

◆ Establish a classroom dynamic where students share their thinking and problem-solving skills on a daily basis. Having children learn from one another can be much more powerful than an environment where the teacher is the sole source of new information and strategies. Students should be encouraged to share their different strategies for solving particular problems, and finding each other's mistakes. If there is no shame in making a mistake because everyone learns from it, children are much more likely to take risks. Consider using the pre-assessments in lieu of one night's homework to lighten your load, and the students' load. A worksheet filled with 30 fraction problems, for example, likely will not provide the same amount of insight into student understanding as the five-concept pre-assessment self-reflection. Both types of homework require time and effort from the students and teachers, but the self-reflection often may be more telling of a student's true level of understanding.

My fellow teachers and I have planned a common assessment on fraction number sense for this coming Friday and today is Monday. I plan on giving the pre-assessment student self-reflection today (Monday) to get an early measurement on my individual students' progress, as well as get an idea of whole-class issues and misunderstandings. My colleagues and I created the pre-assessment self-reflection weeks ago when we were mapping out the fraction number sense unit; we also made the common assessment at the same time so we knew exactly where we needed to be two weeks into the fraction unit. We used the state standards to determine what our students needed to know and worked backward from there. We knew the students needed to be able to identify fractions, find equivalent fractions for bench-mark fractions, compare fractions and order them. Those four standards are what we have spent the last two weeks working on with the students and those are what will be on the test on Friday. We have decided to do a 12-question assessment. Three problems will focus on identifying fractions in the pictorial and number forms, three questions will ask students to find equivalencies, three questions will require students to compare fractions and the final three questions will deal with ordering fractions. We have found the asking three questions for each standard is a solid, but not overwhelming, way to get a good read on what the students truly know. Once we created the common assessment, we were able to quickly create the post-assessment student self-reflection, since we just needed to know the number of items on the assessment and determine which follow-up questions we wanted to ask our students.

Here are the sample assessment (Figures 4.1(a–c), and pre- and post-assessment self-reflections used in these examples (Figures 4.2 and 4.3).

While I have a couple of very quick quizzes and "exit pass" problems to try to get a read on my students' understanding of fraction number sense, I'm still a little fuzzy on who really gets what concepts and who is still struggling; it's hard to always know who knows what and who is really good at just flying under the radar. Needless to say, I'm eager to see their pre-assessment self-reflections to really get a sense for where each of my students is and where they lie as a whole group.

On Monday, I pass out the pre-assessment self-reflections and tell the students to complete them for homework. There is no other math homework.

On Tuesday morning, I collect the pre-assessment self-reflections. Those students who do not have their self-reflections (because they forgot it, were absent Monday or chose not to complete it) will need to miss a few minutes of recess to complete it or complete it during math class today. Having a pre-assessment self-reflection for each of my students is absolutely necessary, so

Name _____ Date _____

Fraction Number Sense

1. What fraction of the rectangles below is shaded?

Answer: _____

2.   Maria bought 12 eggs, but 1 was cracked. What fraction of the eggs was cracked?

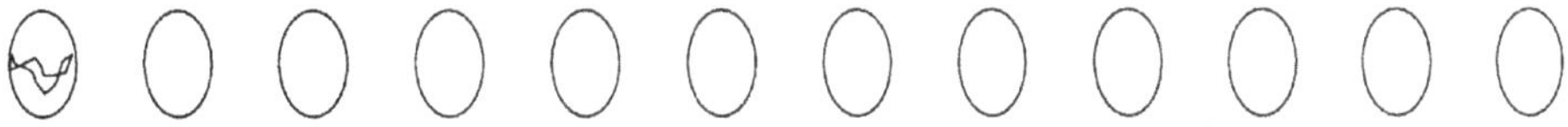

Answer: _____

3.   What fraction of the rectangle is shaded?

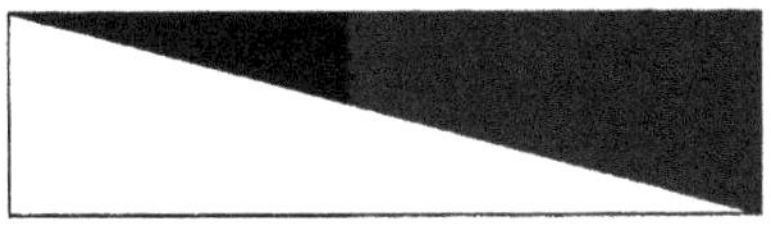

Answer: _____

4.   Allison is making a cake that requires $\frac{1}{2}$ cup of water. Her measuring cup doesn't have $\frac{1}{2}$ labeled. What are 2 fractions that are equivalent to $\frac{1}{2}$ that she might look for instead?

Figure 4.1 The assessment.

5. Jeremiah needed to drill a hole that is $\frac{3}{4}$ inch. What are 2 equivalent fractions

   to $\frac{3}{4}$ that Jeremiah could use to find a bit to drill his hole?

6. What are 3 fractions that are equivalent to: $\frac{4}{5}$?

7. Compare the following fractions using <, > or = $\frac{7}{8}$ _____ $\frac{9}{10}$

8. Compare the following fractions using <, > or = $\frac{3}{10}$ _____ $\frac{5}{10}$

9. Belinda and Erik love to exercise. Belinda walked $\frac{3}{5}$ of a mile yesterday and

   Erik walked $\frac{4}{10}$ of a mile. Who walked farther?

Figure 4.1 (Continued)

10. Put the following fractions in order from LEAST to GREATEST:

$$\frac{1}{2} \qquad \frac{7}{8} \qquad \frac{9}{10} \qquad \frac{3}{4}$$

11. Put the following fractions in order from LEAST to GREATEST:

$$\frac{5}{6} \qquad \frac{1}{3} \qquad \frac{4}{5} \qquad \frac{11}{12}$$

12. DeShawn made a table of the amount of time he spent reading on Sunday, Monday, Tuesday and Wednesday. Put the values in order from LEAST to GREATEST.

Day of the Week	Time Spent Reading (in Hours)
Sunday	$\frac{3}{4}$
Monday	$\frac{1}{2}$
Tuesday	$\frac{1}{4}$
Wednesday	$\frac{5}{6}$

Figure 4.1 (Continued)

Name _____ Date _____

Fraction Number Sense
Pre-Assessment Student Self-Reflection

Concept or Sample Question	DO YOU UNDERSTAND THIS CONCEPT?		
*Which fraction of triangles is shaded? △ ▲ △	YES --------->	Explain:	
	NO, but I am going to do this to help my understanding	Review past assignments/notes Draw picture	ask a friend or family member other: _____ _____
*List 3 equivalent fractions to $\frac{2}{3}$	YES --------->	Explain:	
	NO, but I am going to do this to help my understanding	Review past assignments/notes Draw picture	ask a friend or family member other: _____ _____
*Compare using <, > or = $\frac{1}{3}$ —— $\frac{3}{4}$	YES --------->	Explain:	
	NO, but I am going to do this to help my understanding	Review past assignments/notes Draw picture	ask a friend or family member other: _____ _____
*Order these fractions from LEAST to GREATEST: $\frac{1}{2}, \frac{2}{8}, \frac{1}{10}$	YES --------->	Explain:	
	NO, but I am going to do this to help my understanding	Review past assignments/notes Draw picture	ask a friend or family member other: _____ _____

Figure 4.2 Pre-assessment self-reflection.

Name _____ Date_____

Fraction Number Sense
Post-Assessment Student Self-Reflection

Put a check next to each number that describes how you feel about it.
Remember, this is between you and me; be honest.

Question Number	It is Very Easy	I Feel Pretty Good About This	I Could Use Some More Help	I Need A LOT More Help	I Have No Idea What the Question is Asking of Me
1					
2					
3.					
4.					
5.					
6.					
7.					
8.					
9.					
10.					
11.					
12.					

What part of the test did you think was easiest?

_____

_____

_____

What part of the test was most challenging for you?

_____

_____

_____

You should have checked your work before turning it in. Please tell me which numbers, if any, you were able to correct because you checked your work.

_____

_____

_____

Figure 4.3 Post-assessment self-reflection.

I'll need to carve out a time during the school day today for those students to complete the reflections.

It is Tuesday after school and I now have time to analyze my math students' pre-assessment self-reflections.

I start with Ben's self-reflection first (Figure 4.4). I plan on spending about one minute reviewing each student's pre-assessment self-reflection—about

Name **Ben**   Date_____

Fraction Number Sense
Pre-Assessment Student Self-Reflection

Concept or Sample Question	DO YOU UNDERSTAND THIS CONCEPT?	
* Which fraction of triangles is shaded? △ ▲ △	(YES --------->)	Explain: $\frac{1}{3}$ because the middle triangle is shaded and the other two are white
	NO, but I am going to do this to help my understanding	Review past assignments/ notes ask a friend or family member Draw picture other: _____
* List 3 equivalent fractions to $\frac{2}{3}$	(YES --------->)	Explain: $\frac{2}{3} \times \boxed{\frac{2}{2}} = \frac{4}{6}$ $\frac{2}{3} \times \boxed{\frac{4}{4}} = \frac{8}{12}$ $\frac{2}{3} \times \boxed{\frac{3}{3}} = \frac{6}{9}$ secret agent one
	NO, but I am going to do this to help my understanding	Review past assignments/ notes ask a friend or family member Draw picture other: _____
* Compare using < , > or = $\frac{1}{3}$ __ $\frac{3}{4}$	(YES --------->)	Explain: $\frac{4}{12} \times \boxed{\frac{4}{4}} \times \frac{1}{3}$? $\frac{3}{4} \times \boxed{\frac{3}{3}} = \frac{9}{12}$ $\frac{4}{12} < \frac{9}{12}$ I made both fractions have 12 as denominator
	NO, but I am going to do this to help my understanding	Review past assignments/ notes ask a friend or family member Draw picture other: _____
* Order these fractions from LEAST to GREATEST $\frac{1}{2}, \frac{2}{8}, \frac{1}{10}$	YES ---------> (I think so)	Explain: $\frac{4}{8} = \boxed{\frac{4}{4}} \times \frac{1}{2}$ — $\frac{2}{8} \times \boxed{\frac{1}{1}} = \frac{2}{8}$ $\frac{1}{2} > \frac{1}{10}$ $\frac{4}{8} > \frac{2}{8}$ this is bigger because the pieces are bigger $\frac{1}{2}$ is the biggest
	NO, but I am going to do this to help my understanding	Review past assignments/ notes ask a friend or family member Draw picture other: _____

Figure 4.4 Ben's pre-assessment self-reflection.

what I would spend grading a normal homework sheet. I notice that Ben, who is quite gifted in math, has answered that he understands three of the four concepts (identifying fractions, equivalent fractions, comparing fractions) and has detailed examples to demonstrate his understanding. The 4th concept, however, ordering fractions, seems to have given him a bit a trouble. His thinking is valid, but he seems to be stuck putting together all of his work into the form of an answer. He compared two fractions at a time, which is a strategy we have talked about in class, but he doesn't necessarily know how to extract the information from all of his hard work to properly order the three fractions.

Next, I move on to Carmen's pre-assessment self-reflection. She is a student who usually has little background knowledge in new math concepts but makes connections quickly. She appears to struggle with comparing fractions and ordering fractions, but convinces me that she has grasped identifying fractions and finding equivalent fractions. It is a little troubling for me to see her picture representations of 1/3 and 3/4 for the third objective, so I'll have to make a note to spend some time with her reviewing the concept of equal-sized pieces and wholes (Figure 4.5).

Finally, I take a few minutes to review Ryan's pre-assessment self-reflection. Ryan, who often struggles with math, seems to be struggling with all of the fraction concepts. He marked that he understands identifying fractions, but I see that he made the common mistake of making the denominator the number of unshaded pieces, rather than the total number pieces. He also seems to have a very superficial understanding of equivalences based on his examples and the fact that there is no verbiage or computation to support how he found these equivalences. As I continue to analyze his pre-assessment self-reflection, I'm not convinced that he truly grasps any of the fraction number sense concepts. I see that he is using the cross-multiplication trick that a student shared in class one day, but there doesn't seem to be any evidence that he understands the value of the fractions he is comparing (Figure 4.6).

I continue to analyze the remainder of my students' pre-assessment self-reflections and put them into best-fit groups using a simple chart (Figure 4.7)

Here is what I determine to do using the information on the chart.

Group 1: (students requiring help with all fraction number sense concepts) Ryan + others like Ryan

Group 2: (students requiring help with equivalent fractions and ordering fractions) others

Name __Carmen__   Date_____

Fraction Number Sense
Pre-Assessment Student Self-Reflection

Concept or Sample Question	DO YOU UNDERSTAND THIS CONCEPT?	
* Which fraction of triangles is shaded? △ ▲ △	YES ------>	Explain: $\frac{1}{3}$ is black and 2 are white
	NO, but I am going to do this to help my understanding	Review past assignments/ notes ask a friend or family member Draw picture other: _____
* List 3 equivalent fractions to $\frac{2}{3}$	YES ------>	Explain: $\frac{2}{3} \times \frac{3}{3} = \frac{6}{9}$ $\frac{2}{3} \times \frac{5}{5} = \frac{10}{15}$ $\frac{2}{3} \times \frac{6}{6} = \frac{20}{30}$
	NO, but I am going to do this to help my understanding	Review past assignments/ notes ask a friend or family member Draw picture other: _____
* Compare using <, > or = $\frac{1}{3} \underline{\quad} \frac{3}{4}$	YES ------>	Explain: $\frac{1}{3} < \frac{3}{4}$
	NO, but I am going to do this to help my understanding	Review past assignments/ notes ask a friend or family member Draw picture other: _____
* Order these fractions from LEAST to GREATEST: $\frac{1}{2}, \frac{2}{8}, \frac{1}{10}$	YES ------> NO, but I am going to do this to help my understanding	Explain: I looked but it is still too hard Review past assignments/ notes ask a friend or family member Draw picture other: _____

Figure 4.5 Carmen's pre-assessment self-reflection.

Name _Ryan_ _____ Date_____

Fraction Number Sense
Pre-Assessment Student Self-Reflection

Concept or Sample Question	DO YOU UNDERSTAND THIS CONCEPT?	
* Which fraction of triangles is shaded? △ ▲ △	YES (circled) --------->	Explain: $\frac{1}{2}$ because 1 is dark and 2 are white
	NO, but I am going to do this to help my understanding	Review past assignments/ notes ask a friend or family member Draw picture other: _____ _____
* List 3 equivalent fractions to $\frac{2}{3}$	YES (circled) -------->	Explain: $\frac{20}{30}$, $\frac{200}{300}$, $\frac{2,000}{3,000}$ $\frac{4}{6}$
	NO, but I am going to do this to help my understanding	Review past assignments/ notes ask a friend or family member Draw picture other: _____
* Compare using < , > or = $\frac{1}{3}$ __ $\frac{3}{4}$	YES --------->	Explain: $\frac{1}{3} \times \frac{3}{4}$ 9 is bigger than 4 so $\frac{3}{4}$ 4 9 is bigger than $\frac{1}{3}$
	NO (circled) but I am going to do this to help my understanding	Review past assignments/ notes ask a friend or family member (underlined) Draw picture my mom other: _____ now I know
* Order these fractions from LEAST to GREATEST: $\frac{1}{2}$, $\frac{2}{8}$, $\frac{1}{10}$	YES --------->	Explain: ? ? ? ? ? ? ?
	NO (circled), but I am going to do this to help my understanding	Review past assignments/ notes ask a friend or family member Draw picture other: I need help from you

Figure 4.6 Ryan's pre-assessment self-reflection.

Student Name	Concept 1: Identifying Fractions **Remediation Required**	Concept 2: Equivalent Fractions **Remediation Required**	Concept 3: Comparing Fractions **Remediation Required**	Concept 4: Ordering Fractions **Remediation Required**
Ben				x
Carmen			x	x
Ryan	x	x	x	x

Figure 4.7 Analyzing the self-reflections and grouping students.

Group 3:   (students requiring help with comparing fractions and ordering fractions) Carmen + others

Group 4:   (students who struggle with just ordering fractions) Ben + others

I quickly notice that almost all of my students, even Ben, who excels in math, are struggling with ordering fractions. This is a loud and clear message that I did not cover this concept clearly and I have two days (Wednesday and Thursday) to revisit it before the exam. This will be a whole-class discussion as most of my students appear to need help with it.

The other small-group lessons will be catered to the needs of the students. For instance, Ryan will spend time with me in a small group working with identifying and equivalent fractions. I'll ask Mr. X to focus his small-group lessons comparing fractions (both Ryan and Carmen will visit Mr. X's groups). Students like Ben, who are ready for extensions in all areas except ordering, will meet with me briefly, work in pairs and then be part of the whole-group discussion of ordering fractions. Managing all of the groups is easy once I lay out everything in a table, and get the students accustomed to small-group rotations (Figure 4.8).

Organizing the students like this allows me to meet the needs of each of my students before the assessment has even taken place.

Ryan (Group 1), who represents the students who need the most help, has an opportunity to meet with Mr. X and me in two different, small-group settings, and then be part of the larger whole-class discussion on ordering fractions.

Group 2 works independently for a short time, then joins the second half of my small group focused on equivalences. They then work independently or in partners until the whole-class discussion. Keep in mind, however, that I am circulating through the classroom through much of the period asking and answering questions, so rarely is there a time when the students in this group are truly without teacher support.

Math Class (Wednesday) (9:00-10:00)			
9:00-9:03	Explain who is in each group and where each group will begin. Explain individual/group work assignments. Students rotate to their respective groups and/or work stations.		
9:03-9:18	Group 1– (includes Ryan) works with me on Identifying fractions and finding equivalences	Group 2 –works independently, then joins the 2nd part of group 1's discussion on equivalences	Group 3 – (includes Carmen) works with Mr. X on comparing fractions	Group 4 – (includes Ben) Independent work and/or Partner work
9:18-9:21	Students rotate to new groups and/or work stations. Group 4 checks in with Mr. X or me to report progress.		
9:21-9:36	Group 1 (includes Ryan) goes to Mr. X to work on comparing fractions	Groups 2 + 3 – check in with me, then work independently or in partners. I use remainder of time to work with students individually or part of any group that requires assistance.		
9:36-9:40	Students return to their seats to prepare for whole class discussion		
9:40-10:00	Whole Class discussion about Ordering (all students), led by me, as Mr. X circulates and helps students individually		

Figure 4.8 Small-group rotations.

Carmen's group (Group 3) begins by working with Mr. X and then, like Group 2, works independently or in partnerships, until the whole-class discussion.

Ben's group (Group 4) is mainly on its own; however, they are responsible for reporting their progress at several times throughout the period and have access to teacher support for the majority of the period as I circulate around the classroom. They, too, join the whole-class discussion on ordering fractions.

For Thursday, I meet briefly with Mr. X to discuss his thoughts on student progress, and we set up a similar whole-class/small-group/independent work rotation system. Our goal is to have each student leave class on Thursday with the gaps in her fraction number sense understanding fully filled in.

NO BACKUP?

The preceding scenario assumes that there is at least one other adult teacher available to take a small group, but we know that this is not always the case. So, what happens if you are the sole teacher and your students need varying levels of support and remediation? A couple of suggestions:

◆ Partner students with opposite strengths and have them work with one another. For example, create a group with one or two students who have mastered ordering fractions with one or two students who struggle with ordering fractions. Have them play games and/or do practice problems. The students who already know the material will reinforce it for one another—teaching is a great way to master a concept—and will help those students who need more remediation. Several fluid groups are necessary to meet all of the students' needs. You, as the teacher, would rotate around checking progress, challenging and remediating where necessary.

◆ Have several independent work stations—either computer/tablet-based or pen/paper where students can work on reinforcing concepts while you pull as many small groups as possible.

◆ Determine if it is possible to work with another teacher or group of teachers to group similarly-skilled students. This will increase the number of students, but it also increases the number of teachers and classrooms available to pull small groups.

◆ Ask for help from resource teachers or assistant teachers in the building—perhaps the math specialist or special education teacher can offer assistance during the week leading up an assessment, if not each class meeting.

My teaching team and I each give the common assessment to our respective classes on Friday, and also require that the students fill out the post-assessment self-reflection before turning in their test. Because we have chosen to give a smaller 12-question test, there are no issues with students lacking sufficient time to complete the test and the post-assessment self-reflection.

Over the weekend, I analyze the tests and see how they correspond to the students' post-assessment self-reflections.

It seems both Ben and Carmen feel confident about fraction number sense; their test results are very high and their post-assessment self-reflections indicate that they feel confident in their own abilities as well. The post-assessment self-reflection is tangible evidence of students building confidence in their own math abilities.

Ryan's test results and post-assessment self-reflection are a little more complicated. He marked that he feels really good about questions 1–9 and guessed on questions 10–12. While Ryan did do quite well on questions 1–6 (identifying fractions and finding equivalent fractions), he answered questions 8 and 9 incorrectly on the test. These were two of the three questions dealing with comparing fractions; number 7 was the third question focused on comparing fractions and he answered that one correctly, although his picture does not represent the fractions accurately. This is so interesting and valuable because, according to the post-assessment self-reflection, Ryan clearly feels as though he understands how to compare fractions. However, the test results say something entirely different. Ryan does not know that he does not know how to correctly do this—a fact that may have been lost without the aid of the post-assessment self-reflection. How can we expect Ryan to really care about intervention and remediation centered around the concept of comparing fractions when he incorrectly believes that he already knows how to do this? When given an opportunity during an intervention window to play a game or choose an activity that might help Ryan compare fractions, like "Fraction War," Ryan would not even know to consider that option because he thinks he has mastered the concept of comparing fractions.

Ryan also missed questions 10 and 12 on the test, which dealt with ordering fractions; he answered number 11 correctly (also an ordering fractions question) (Figure 4.9(a–c)). However, according to the post-assessment self-reflection, for the ordering fractions questions, Ryan recognized that he guessed on these questions, which indicates to me that he does not feel comfortable with this particular concept and still needs more assistance (Figure 4.10).

On Monday, as the students are filing in and getting settled, I pull Ryan aside for a very quick chat meant to focus on a positive aspect of his assessment and reflection—the value of him checking his work. I mention that he got question 6 right, even though he had the wrong answer initially. When I looked back at the work that he originally wrote versus what he ended up writing, I learned a lot. He first added 2/2 to 4/5 instead of multiplying by 2/2. This may mean that he is relying too heavily on an algorithm rather than truly understanding the value of the numbers. I need to keep an eye on this. In any event, this quick discussion between the two of us, recognizing the value of Ryan's checking over his own work takes just a minute, and helps him to see that he would have gotten 7/12 instead of 8/12 on the test. While I can tell that Ryan is upset by his grade, it is nice for him to know that his double-checking of his work helped his score, and, more importantly, helped him see his own mistakes, correct them, and learn from them (*see Vignette 5, Chapter 6 for the quick discussion between Ryan and Mrs. Z*).

Today (Monday) and tomorrow (Tuesday), Mr. X and I have decided to divide the students based on their test and post-assessment reflection results. Earlier in the semester, my fellow teachers and I had tentatively said that we would start the next section of our fractions unit today, but we have decided

Name __Ryan_____ Date_____

Fraction Number Sense

1. What fraction of the rectangles below is shaded?

■	■	■	□
1	2	3	4

Answer: $\dfrac{3 \text{ shaded}}{4 \text{ totol}}$

2. Maria bought 12 eggs, but 1 was cracked. What fraction of the eggs was cracked?

1 2 3 4 5 6 7 8 9 10 11 12

Answer: $\dfrac{1 \text{ cracked}}{12 \text{ totol}}$

3. What fraction of the rectangle is shaded?

1

2

Answer: $\dfrac{1 \text{ black}}{2 \text{ totol}}$

4. Allison is making a cake that requires $\frac{1}{2}$ cup of water. Her measuring cup doesn't have $\frac{1}{2}$ labeled. What are 2 fractions that are equivalent to $\frac{1}{2}$ that she might look for instead?

$$\frac{1}{2} \times \frac{2}{2} = \frac{2}{4}$$

$$\frac{1}{2} \times \frac{3}{3} = \frac{3}{6}$$

and I know 3 is half of 6 and 2 is half of 4

Figure 4.9 (a) Ryan's test (p. 1); (b) Ryan's test (p. 2); (c) Ryan's test (p. 3).

5. Jeremiah needed to drill a hole that is $\frac{3}{4}$ inch. What are 2 equivalent fractions

to $\frac{3}{4}$ that Jeremiah could use to find a bit to drill his hole?

$4 \times 1 = 4$
$4 \times 2 = 8$

$$\frac{3}{4} \times \frac{2}{2} = \frac{6}{8}$$

$3 \times 1 = 3$
$3 \times 2 = 6$
$3 \times 3 = 9$ $3 \times 4 = 12$

$$\frac{3}{4} \times \frac{3}{3} = \frac{9}{12}$$

6. What are 3 fractions that are equivalent to: $\frac{4}{5}$?

$4 \times 1 = 4$
$4 \times 2 = 8$
$4 \times 3 = 12$
$4 \times 4 = 16$
$4 \times 5 = 20$

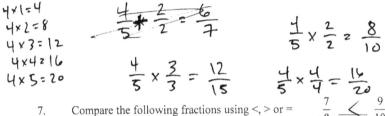

$$\frac{4}{5} \times \frac{2}{2} = \frac{6}{7}$$

$$\frac{4}{5} \times \frac{2}{2} = \frac{8}{10}$$

$$\frac{4}{5} \times \frac{3}{3} = \frac{12}{15}$$

$$\frac{4}{5} \times \frac{4}{4} = \frac{16}{20}$$

7. Compare the following fractions using <, > or = $\quad \frac{7}{8} \; < \; \frac{9}{10}$

8. Compare the following fractions using <, > or = $\quad \frac{3}{10} \; > \; \frac{5}{10}$

$$\frac{5}{10} \; > \; \frac{3}{10}$$

$50 \qquad 30$

9. Belinda and Erik love to exercise. Belinda walked $\frac{3}{5}$ of a mile yesterday and

Erik walked $\frac{4}{10}$ of a mile. Who walked farther?

$$\frac{3}{10} = \frac{2}{2} \times \frac{3}{5} - \frac{4}{10}$$

$$\frac{3}{10} < \frac{4}{10}$$

Figure 4.9 (Continued)

10.   Put the following fractions in order from LEAST to GREATEST:

$$\frac{1}{2} \qquad \frac{7}{8} \qquad \frac{9}{10} \qquad \frac{3}{4}$$

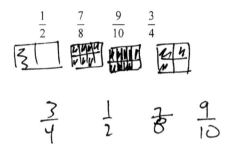

$$\frac{3}{4} \qquad \frac{1}{2} \qquad \frac{7}{8} \qquad \frac{9}{10}$$

11.   Put the following fractions in order from LEAST to GREATEST:

$$\frac{5}{6} \qquad \frac{1}{3} \qquad \frac{4}{5} \qquad \frac{11}{12}$$

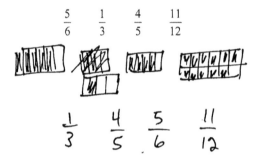

$$\frac{1}{3} \qquad \frac{4}{5} \qquad \frac{5}{6} \qquad \frac{11}{12}$$

12.   DeShawn made a table of the amount of time he spent reading on Sunday, Monday, Tuesday and Wednesday. Put the values in order from LEAST to GREATEST.

Day of the Week	Time Spent Reading (in Hours)
Sunday	$\frac{3}{4} \times \frac{2}{2} = \frac{6}{8}$
Monday	$\frac{1}{2} \times \frac{2}{2} = \frac{2}{4}$
Tuesday	$\frac{1}{4} \times \frac{2}{2} = \frac{2}{8}$
Wednesday	$\frac{5}{6} \times \frac{2}{2} = \frac{10}{12}$

$$\frac{1}{2} \qquad \frac{1}{4} \qquad \frac{5}{6} \qquad \frac{3}{4}$$

Figure 4.9 (Continued)

Name __Ryan_____ Date_____

Fraction Number Sense
Post-Assessment Student Self-Reflection

Put a check next to each number that describes how you feel about it.
Remember, this is between you and me; be honest.

Question Number	It is Very Easy	I Feel Pretty Good About This	I Could Use Some More Help	I Need A LOT More Help	I Have No Idea What the Question is Asking of Me
1	✓				
2	✓				
3.	✓				
4.	✓				
5.	✓				
6.	✓				
7.	✓				
8.	✓				
9.	✓				
10.	✓			✓	
11.				✓	
12.				✓	

What part of the test did you think was easiest?

_____numbers 1-6 were so easy_____

_____

_____

What part of the test was most challenging for you?

_____just 10-12_____

_____

_____

You should have checked your work before turning it in. Please tell me which numbers, if any, you were able to correct because you checked your work.

_____#6 because I added 2/2 instead_____

_____of timesing it_____

_____

Figure 4.10 Ryan's post-assessment self-reflection.

to push that back a few days to give us some time to try to fill in gaps for those students still missing key components of the first part of our fractions unit. There seems to be little point in moving on when a good number of students are still struggling with comparing and ordering fractions. Those students who have mastered the concepts covered on the assessment will be challenged with enrichment concepts. Those who struggle will work with Mr. X and me to fill in the gaps.

WHO HAS TIME FOR ALL OF THIS *EXTRA* ANALYSIS? NOT ME!

I imagine the knee-jerk reaction to these ideas from many teachers is "No, thanks. I don't need anything else to do." I would urge you to just try the self-reflections in some capacity—either pre- or post-test—to see if you change your mind.

Admittedly, it will take some work to make the templates and walk your students through the processes. That said, I believe that, ultimately, it will save you and your students time, as well as build confidence in your students. How? By using the pre-assessment self-reflections you are dialing in on exactly who needs what remediation. Rather than doing whole-class reviews on concepts that a majority of your students already know, you can focus your time and energy on small groups that need different areas of support. If you receive your students' pre-assessment self-reflections a few days before the assessment, you can sort them into groups and spend the days leading up to the assessment meeting each student's specific needs. Ideally, this will mean that there are fewer days lost to teaching kids what they already know before the assessment, and fewer days lost to remediation after the assessment because you had the necessary information to intervene before the assessment even took place. By using the post-assessment self-reflections, you can determine exactly which students are ready to move on and exactly which ones need more time with the current topics. The "lucky guessers" are identified, the kids who are honest about not understanding certain concepts can be given specific help, and the ones who have mastered the material can move on.

If this larger process seems daunting right now, one way to try to incorporate a smaller-scale student self-reflection is to simply add this type of checklist table at the bottom of each homework page, worksheet and assessment. A similar table could be added to the side of—or after—each question as well.

STOP	Circle the choice that best describes how you felt about answering the questions above:		
	The questions were:	EASY	HARD, BUT I THINK I GOT IT	I GUESSED

This will require a bit of explaining to your students, and it is not nearly as thorough as the exhaustive pre- and post-assessment student self-reflections, but it will allow you, the teacher, to glean some data on student understanding. For instance, if the student marks that the questions were "easy," and got most/all of the questions right, the student has likely mastered the material. If he marked that they were "easy" and got every question wrong, the student clearly does not understand the material, nor does he feel like he needs help—even though he does. This student might be the one who says he is ready for the test and would prefer to read or play games on the days leading up to the test instead of reviewing the material. In reality, he needs remediation and this can be done before the assessment. The student who says "Hard But I Think I Got It" may recognize the content as challenging, and may or may not have mastered it. Looking quickly back at his right/wrong ratio will help you determine if he truly does have a grasp on the content at hand. If he admitted that he "guessed" then it is quite clear that more instruction is needed. Either way, you have a bit more information that what you would have if there were no reflection questions at all.

5

From the Parent's Perspective

So often teachers hear that parents want to take an active role in helping their children succeed but aren't quite sure how to go about it. Some of them fear that assisting with homework is enabling too much, or that the methods they learned back in school are too outdated to be of any help to their children. I even hear quite frequently that parents don't really know what their children are learning in school at any given time, so it is nearly impossible for them to lend a helping hand. The pre- and post-assessment self-reflections can be very helpful to parents in getting a sense of what their children are required to know, where their children stand before the assessment and what their children's level of understanding is after the assessment. The remainder of this chapter is written from the perspective of Ryan's mother. She knows that Ryan struggles with math, but until this year and the introduction of the self-reflections, she has really felt helpless as to how to improve his skills and confidence.

It is Monday evening and Ryan mentioned that he has a math test this Friday. He has been working on the pre-assessment self-reflection for the past 30 minutes and I asked to see it when he finishes.

After looking at the pre-assessment self-reflection, I understand that Ryan is having a hard time with identifying fractions, comparing and ordering them. I remember when I was in school, I also had a hard time with comparing and ordering fractions, and to be honest, I still don't know that I really "get it". So, I told Ryan that I would ask some of my coworkers about it tomorrow.

DOI: 10.4324/9781003329176-5

I remember a trick I learned 20 years ago multiplying the top number by the bottom number of the other fraction and using that to help you figure out which one is bigger, so I showed him that, but I don't know if that is all that helpful because it is just a trick and doesn't really help clarify the value of the numbers.

We also spent a lot of time identifying fractions. I draw a bunch of pictures, circles, squares, rectangles and we talked about how the total number of pieces is the denominator and the ones being asked about where the numerator. We even played a game with playing cards that Ryan taught me from his class. He won three times in a row!

Today is Tuesday and I feel like I can help Ryan a little bit more with comparing and ordering fractions after talking with my coworkers about it and looking on the internet for suggestions, although I'm not totally comfortable taking on the role of the teacher. Ryan and I played the card game tonight again that his teacher sent home, and I suggested he ask his favorite 3rd grade teacher, Mrs. B to help him with comparing and ordering fractions. He got sort of embarrassed, and said he'd think about it. He said that his current teacher and Mr. X were going to help him. So, we made a date to play the identifying fraction card game Wednesday and Thursday night. I sent an email to his teacher letting her know that we are playing the game where we identify the fractions, but that I'm probably not too much help when it comes to comparing fractions. I asked her to provide extra help to Ryan, since I think she will do a better job than I will. I also asked if she had any websites with games or videos that I could use with Ryan at home.

It's Friday afternoon and I asked Ryan how the math test went at school today. He said three of the problems on ordering fractions were really hard, but he though the rest of them were so easy! I'm so happy to hear that he thinks he "aced" the test!

Today is Monday and Ryan brought his test and post-assessment self-reflection home. The great news was that it seems the identifying fractions game we played was a help because he got all of those questions right! However, he did miss 4 of the 12 problems. I wasn't too surprised to see that Ryan had a tough time with the two questions about ordering fractions, but I was a little shocked to see that he also missed two problems dealing with comparing fractions. Ryan said that he was also surprised because he thought he had answered those questions correctly. He was a little bummed to get a C on the test, but it was very helpful for both of us to see that he has a tough time with comparing and ordering fractions still.

Ryan and I looked closely at the four questions that he missed and he explained to me why he missed each of them. We figured out the correct answers together, but I've also asked my cousin, who has always been great in math, to come over to help Ryan. I want her to see the post-assessment self-reflection and the test, so she can help Ryan with similar problems. Ryan also mentioned that his teacher is having him spend extra time on comparing and ordering fractions. I know that we don't need to spend quite as much time playing the fraction card game where he and I take turns identifying fractions from pictures—he seems to have that down very well. Instead, I looked on the internet and found another game that we can play that deals with comparing and ordering fractions. I also found a couple of 3- and 5-minute videos about comparing and ordering fractions that we can watch together.

SUGGESTIONS FOR PARENTS

◆ Ask your child often about their schoolwork, using open-ended questions that require them to give detailed answers, instead of answering "yes" or "no"

◆ Make homework discussions, and reviewing pre- and post-assessment self-reflections a regular routine

◆ Do not hesitate to contact your child's teacher to ask for progress reports, and/or additional resources to help your child, especially if the content is unfamiliar to you

◆ Reach out to other parents to form network that shares ideas, strategies, information and resources

◆ Have your child make "quizzes" for you that she reviews and grades. The process of her making questions and then grading the answers is incredibly powerful for solidifying content

◆ Have your child write a story, draw a picture, sing a song, make up a dance or play describing what he is doing on class

◆ Create and host "study groups" that involve other students and parents in a fun, social setting; the more kids enjoy learning, the more they learn

◆ Use idle time (i.e. in the car or in line at the grocery store) to ask your child questions about current content, as well as previously-learned material (i.e. "My gas tank is one quarter full. How many quarters of gas have I used since I last filled it up?")

◆ Use the internet to help you! There are many videos and websites available that show step-by-step instructions on most, if not all, mathematical concepts. Watch a couple of them—with your child or on your own. Even if you are unable to help your child, watching a video with him gives the message that you value school and his success.

6

Snapshots from the Classroom

Vignette 1: The Pre-Assessment Reflection

MRS. Z: *All right, girls and boys, tonight for homework, your job is to complete the decimals pre-assessment self-reflection. As I have mentioned in the past, this is to help you, your parents and me get a good idea of what you know already and what you are still working on mastering. If there is something on here that is difficult for you, it is your responsibility to get assistance. You can ask me for help. Mr. X is also here to help. Your friends and family, or even your notebook, may be great resources. Remember that everything that is on this pre-assessment self-reflection is similar to what you will see on our test on Friday.*

MARIA: [later that day, thinking to herself as she begins the pre-assessment self-reflection] *The question asks me to list decimals and fractions in order from least to greatest, but I can never remember if 1/10 or 0.01 is bigger. I am going to circle "Ask a friend or family member" and see if my sister can help me. She is really good at math.*

MARIA (TO HER SISTER, EVELYN): *Ev, I have a test in math on Friday and I need your help. I can't ever remember which number is bigger, this one* (points to 1/10) *or this one* (points to 0.01).

EVELYN: *OK, let's talk this out. The numbers look pretty similar, don't they? But, really, they are very different. Try saying the names of the fractions to see if that helps you figure out which one is bigger.*

MARIA: *So the first one is one-tenth and the second one is one hundredth, right?*

DOI: 10.4324/9781003329176-6

EVELYN: *Uh-huh, yes. Does that help you at all?*

MARIA: *Hmm, well I know that if I had a candy bar and I could have one of ten pieces or one of one hundred pieces, I'd rather have the candy bar broken into ten pieces because those pieces would be a lot bigger. Plus, we talked about how a penny is one part out of a hundred pieces that make a whole dollar, and a dime is one part out of ten pieces that make a whole dollar. I know that a dime is bigger than a penny, so 1/10 must be bigger.*

EVELYN: *YES! Great work!*

MARIA: *OK, thanks, Ev. I'm ready to explain that to my teacher now.*

EVELYN: *Well, hold on, let's do one more practice problem like that ... just to make sure. Then you can write that first example and the second down for you (and your teacher) to see over and over again.*

Vignette 2: The Pre-Assessment Reflection

MRS. Z: *All right, girls and boys, tonight for homework, your job is to complete the decimals pre-assessment self-reflection. As I have mentioned in the past, this is to help you, your parents and me get a good idea of what you know already and what you are still working on mastering. If there is something on here that is difficult for you, it is your responsibility to get assistance. Mr. X is also here to help. Your friends and family, or even your notebook with old problems and homework may be great resources. Other good options for helping you review information are the flashcards that we made last week and the website XYZ. Remember that everything that is on this pre-assessment self-reflection is similar to what you will see on our test on Friday. If you have a question or are not totally clear on the items that are on the pre-assessment self-reflection, now is the time to let me, Mr. Z or your parents know. There are still four days before the assessment, which means we have a lot of time to review!*

ANDREW: [later that day, thinking to himself as he begins the pre-assessment self-reflection] *The question asks me to list decimals and fractions in order from least to greatest, but I can never remember if 1/10 or 0.01 is bigger. Mr. X taught us this really cool way to turn all decimals into fractions by just saying the name of the decimal aloud, but I need to look at my notes from that day to really get it stuck in my head. I think he also said I should write both numbers as fractions, or both numbers as decimals, because that makes it easier to compare. I think I know how to do this, but I am going to circle "Look at my notes" to make sure that I understand how to do this, and then I can go back to the pre-assessment reflection and order the decimals, showing my work and thinking.*

Vignette 3: The Pre-Assessment Reflection

Ryan (from Chapter 3) has brought home his pre-assessment self-reflection on Wednesday afternoon. His teacher has already looked at it and decided which small groups and whole-group lessons he will be in for remediation, but he now also has an opportunity to share the results with his mom. She is hesitant in her math ability but willing to reach out the teacher and play games that Ryan has brought home.

RYAN: *Mom, I have my math test on Friday and I'm still not getting fractions.*

MOM: *OK, let's look at the reflection that you did on Monday for homework and see if we can come up with some things we can do together.*

RYAN: *When you helped me on Monday with the problem where I have to compare 1/3 and 3/4 I thought I understood because you showed me that trick, but now I can't remember what I need to do. Is it multiply the 1 times the 4 and then the 3 times the 3, and then what do I do?*

MOM: *Oh, I know—that used to happen to me a lot, too. That trick can be really great when you remember all of the steps, but I don't think it really helps too much with understanding what the numbers really mean. I talked to my coworkers today at work and they all thought that it is better for us to not rely on tricks, but rather use pictures so that we can get a better idea of the fractions. Also, I sent Mrs. Z an email yesterday (Tuesday) asking her if she had any extra math resources that she could send home that might help you with comparing fractions. She said she was going to send something home. Did she give you anything?*

RYAN: *Yes, she gave me more fraction cards that I need to cut and color and she also printed out a list of websites that we can visit together. These fraction cards are a little different from the other ones that we have been using to identify fractions.*

MOM: *OK, let's look at both sets of cards this afternoon. You start working on cutting and coloring the new set of cards and I'll take a look at the websites to see if I can find something that makes sense to me, too. I don't have a lot of time tonight, but I can spend 10 minutes with you right now…*

Vignette 4: The Post-Assessment Reflection

Mrs. Z, her fellow 5th grade teachers and Mr. X are meeting briefly on Monday morning to chat about whole-class trends they noticed from the post-assessment and associated self-reflection.

MRS. Z: *I know the kids will be here any minute but I wanted to touch base with everyone about the fractions test last Friday and your class's results. What were the big takeaways from the assessment and post-assessment reflections in your classes?*

MR. R: *Overall, I think my students mastered identifying fractions, finding equivalent fractions, and comparing fractions, but I had 11 kids miss at least two questions of the three questions that dealt with ordering fractions, especially #12.*

MRS. T: *I saw a similar trend in my class. I had 5 kids miss number #10, 8 kids miss number #11 and 12 kids miss #12. Maybe it was the table in #12 that gave them all a hard time? Reflecting on my lessons leading up to the assessment, I realized that I don't think I ever gave them an example where the fractions were presented in a table form. We spent a lot of time talking about ordering fractions in word problems, but never when they were in a table.*

MRS. Z: *Oh, man! I bet that was part of the problem! I saw similar issues with my students struggling to order fractions, but the one problem that most of them missed was #12. Now that you mention it, I'm realizing that I didn't do any examples with tables either. I wonder if that caused the problem to be even more daunting for them.*

MR. R: *Also, I think as they got toward the end of the test, they probably got tired and had less stamina. But, I agree that my students had not had a lot of practice with ordering fractions from a table either.*

MRS. Z: *Can we agree then that we need to spend a couple of more days on ordering fractions before moving on to adding fractions with unlike denominators. I know we had it on the schedule for starting today, but I think our students need more practice. Can you, Mr. R and Mrs. T, create or find a resource during specials that may be helpful with revisiting and reteaching ordering fractions, especially when in table form? Whatever we have been doing in the past does not seem to be resonating with all of our students. Mr. Z. and I will work on creating or finding a related enrichment project for the kids who have shown clear mastery of the concepts.*

In this vignette, the teachers were able to identity whole-class (or really whole-grade) issues that their students were having with ordering fractions. One teacher, in particular, (Mrs. T) also hypothesized—after reflecting on her own teaching methodology—that perhaps her students struggled with ordering fractions that were presented in tables because she had not spent any time working through similarly structured problems in her day-to-day class. In this instance, the teacher's reflection on her own teaching may have uncovered an issue that the teachers need to address before moving on to the next unit of study.

Vignette 5: The Post-Assessment Reflection

Students are filing into the classroom on Monday morning. They took the test on the previous Friday and Ryan's teacher, Mrs. Z, wants to recognize Ryan's effort in checking his work and making corrections before turning in his test.

MRS. Z: *Ryan, can I speak to you for just a sec?*

RYAN: *Sure, Mrs. Z.*

MRS. Z: *Here's your post-assessment student self-reflection from the test on Friday.*

RYAN: *Uh-huh.*

MRS. Z: *Well, Ryan, you mentioned on the bottom of the self-reflection that you changed your answer for question number 6 from 6/7* (which was incorrect) *to 8/10* (which was correct).

RYAN: *Yeah, I saw that when I was checking over my work. When I was trying to find a fraction that was equivalent to 4/5, I just added 2/2 to the numerator and denominator because I wasn't really paying attention. But then, when I went back over it, I thought about 4/5 for a second. How could it be equal to 6/7 when they're both one part away from the whole? I saw that I added 2/2 instead of "timesing" 2/2, so I changed my answer and knew it was right once I did that. I remembered that a number over itself like 2/2 is the same as 1, and when I multiply any number by 1, I'm not changing the value—just renaming it, like when I multiply 4 times 1 it is always still a 4. But if I add 1 to a number, I'm increasing it (like 2 + 1 = 3), so I knew that wasn't the right thing to do since they have to be equal in value.*

MRS. Z: *Ryan, that's wonderful! Do you realize that you would have gotten number 6 wrong and it would have changed your score drastically? You would have gotten just 7/12 answers write on the test instead of 8/12. That makes a huge difference! Plus, it lets me know that you really do know how to find equivalent fractions! Great job!*

While Ryan still needs a lot of help with comparing and ordering fractions, his teacher can feel confident that he understands how to find equivalent fractions.

WHAT DO I DO WITH THE STUDENT WHO WILL NOT TRUTHFULLY REFLECT ON HER LEVEL OF UNDERSTANDING?

What if there is a student who races through the self-reflections marking any and all categories, giving little or no deep thought to their answers repeatedly? This is a tough situation. The primary purpose of the self-reflections is to help students. We are trying to help them identify their strengths, their weaknesses, viable strategies for filling in gaps in their understanding and showing mastery of the material. We, as their teachers, know that, usually, their parents can see that, but for students, it can sometimes be a challenge. How can you help a student who isn't willing to reflect themself on what they need help on? Some suggestions:

◆ Continue to meet with the obstinate student one-on-one and in small groups.
◆ Have other students share success stories about revealing their weaknesses and how getting help ended up making a positive difference.
◆ Schedule a parent–student–teacher conference (in person, online or even on the phone) that has a positive tone, but focuses on the benefit of self-reflection and remediation
◆ Positively reinforce even small steps in the right direction. If the student reveals even just a tiny bit of information that allows you to get a better picture of her understanding, use it to demonstrate how valuable information can be.
◆ Try to uncover the reason(s) for why the student is so reluctant to share. Work with a school counselor or trusted adult to see if the student will share more information with him/her. Maybe the child student has had a bad experience sharing answers aloud in the past and is worried they will be made fun of if they do not know all of the answers all of the time.
◆ Try implementing weekly progress reports that ask students to reflection their understanding and progress on a variety of topics— things like how they feel they did at specials or how well they kept their desks organized—to get them used to reflection. Use the momentum from these "lower-risk" progress reports to move to assessment-specific reflections.

7

Sample Quiz and Reflection Analyses in Math Classes

1st Grade Quiz and Reflection

The examples given earlier in this text center around a 5th grade math class; however the pre- and post-assessment student self-reflections can, and should, be used at most grade levels and subject areas. Here you can see a sample quiz and some sample student reflections and analyses from a 1st grade math class. There were three questions related to change-unknown, three questions related to result-unknown and three questions related to start-unknown problem types.

The post-assessment (Figure 7.1(a and b)) is a very basic table that asks these students (presumably 1st graders) to simply check the box that best describes how they feel about each question—specifically, if they found the question "easy" or "hard." Because the students are young, it is important to keep questions and choices simple and not overly language-heavy. Notice that this teacher has opted not to add any additional reflection prompts after the initial nine-question check (such as "What quiz numbers were most challenging/easiest for you?" or "What questions did you correct after checking your work?").

Now a look at sample student work and reflection (Figure 7.2(a and b)).

Alex did pretty well on this quiz. Out of 9 questions, he answered 7 correctly and 2 incorrectly (#3 and #8). In his post-assessment self-reflection, Alex responded that he found number 3 to be challenging, which is one of the

DOI: 10.4324/9781003329176-7

Name _____ Date_____

Math Quiz
(CCSS.MATH.CONTENT.1.OA.A.)

1. Rob has 14 balls. He loses some balls. Now Rob has 9 balls. How many balls did Rob lose? Show your work.

2. Kim has 9 pennies. She spends 5 pennies. How many pennies does Kim have left? Show your work.

3. Pat has some flowers. She gets 6 more. Now Pat has 20 flowers. How many flowers did Pat start with? Show your work.

Complete each number sentence to make it true.

4. $19 - \_\_\_ = 12$ 7. $4 + \_\_\_\_ = 11$

5. $12 - 7 = \_\_\_\_$ 8. $2 + 15 = \_\_\_\_$

6. $\_\_\_\_ + 9 = 18$ 9. $\_\_\_\_ - 6 = 11$

Figure 7.1 (a and b) Post-assessment and reflection.

A blank sample math quiz and related post-assessment self-reflection for a first grade class.

_____'s Quiz Reflection

How do you think you did on the quiz?
Put a check in the area that describes how you feel about each question.

Question Number	This was easy!	This was hard or I don't know how to do it
1		
2		
3		
4		
5		
6		
7		
8		
9		

Figure 7.1 (Continued)

questions that he missed. He said that all of the other questions were "easy" for him—even though he did answer #8 incorrectly.

A quick look at his quiz shows us that for #3, rather than find the starting quantity of flowers, Alex added the two given numbers together. Given his reflection response that this question was difficult for him, and his corresponding incorrect answer on the quiz, it is clear that Alex needs help with this type of word problem. Alex's teacher probably needs to review the format with him so that he is better prepared to identify and solve a "start-unknown" word problem. What is very important to note is that he answered both of the other "start-unknown" questions (#6 and #9) correctly, so Alex appears to understand the concept, but he needs a review of this type of problem when it is presented as a word problem. Kudos should be given to Alex by his teacher(s) and his parent(s) for honestly responding on the self-reflection that he struggled with this problem.

The other problem that he missed (#8) appears to be a simple computational mistake or careless error, as opposed to lack of conceptual misunderstanding. He got both the word problem, and the other numerical version of this type of problem correct (#2 and #5), and he responded on his self-reflection that he thought he got this one correct as well. His teacher should check with him to get more information and confirm this theory, but it is likely that he just made a simple computational error, given the fact that he answered the other similar questions correctly, and he marked that he is confident with his ability to answer that question.

Name ___Alex_____ Date_____

Math Quiz
(CCSS.MATH.CONTENT.1.OA.A.)

1. Rob has 14 balls. He loses some balls. Now Rob has 9 balls. How many balls did Rob lose? Show your work.

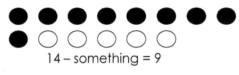

14 – something = 9

14 – 9 = 5 so 14 – 5 = 9

2. Kim has 9 pennies. She spends 5 pennies. How many pennies does Kim have left? Show your work.

4

3. Pat has some flowers. She gets 6 more. Now Pat has 20 flowers. How many flowers did Pat start with? Show your work?

$$20 + 6 = 26 \quad ?????$$

Complete each number sentence to make it true.

4. 19 - _7_ = 12

5. 12 – 7 = _5_

6. _9__ + 9 = 18

7. 4 + _7__ = 11

8. 2 + 15 = _16_

9. _17_ - 6 = 11

Figure 7.2 (a and b) Alex's quiz.

Alex's math quiz and related post-assessment self-reflection showing that he answered two questions incorrectly (#3 and #8), even though he only thought one of the problems (#3) was "hard" or that he didn't "know how to do it".

Based on the assessment and associated reflection, Alex's teacher should probably spend a bit more time with Alex on start-unknown word problems types, and feel confident that he is ready to move on from there.

Beth answered questions #1, #2, #3, #4, #5, and #9 incorrectly (Figure 7.3). She admitted in the post-assessment self-reflection (and by using question

_____Alex___'s Quiz Reflection

How do you think you did on the quiz?
Put a check in the area that describes how you feel about each question.

Question Number	This was easy	This was hard or I don't know how to do it
1	X	
2	X	
3		X
4	X	
5	X	
6	X	
7	X	
8	X	
9	X	

Figure 7.2 (Continued)

marks on the quiz) that she did not know how to answer questions #1 and #3, but she seemed confident in her abilities with all of the other questions (she filled in answers [rather than question marks] on the actual quiz, and also marked "This was easy" on the post-assessment self-reflection). A closer look at Beth's quiz and reflection sheds some light on what is likely Beth's actual level of understanding. She clearly needs more help with the concepts from #1 and #3 **and she knows that**, but she also made computational errors on #2, #4, #5 and #9. However, she thought she answered all of those questions correctly, based on her post-assessment self-reflection. There is a good chance Beth is using some form of an algorithm, but using it incorrectly. For instance, maybe she is counting on or using her fingers, but starting at the wrong number. Her teacher may have been able to help determine the problem before the assessment had she asked Beth to do some of these types of problems in the pre-assessment self-reflection. Because Beth said she feels confident in her ability—and, in reality, she needs more support—she would probably be unlikely to study or spend time preparing for the assessment, or even asking for help from a friend or trusted adult (teacher or parent/caregiver).

A pre-assessment self-reflection could have been very helpful identifying the sources of her misunderstanding and remedying it before the quiz was given. Either way, the post-assessment and the associated reflection clearly show that Beth needs remediation and is not yet ready to move on to math concepts that build off of the ones presented in this quiz. Beth will likely

Name____Beth_____Date_____

Math Quiz

(CCSS.MATH.CONTENT.1.OA.A.)

1. Rob has 14 balls. He loses some balls. Now Rob has 9 balls. How many balls did Rob lose? Show your work.

???

2. Kim has 9 pennies. She spends 5 pennies. How many pennies does Kim have left? Show your work.

$$9 - 5 = 3$$

3. Pat has some flowers. She gets 6 more. Now Pat has 20 flowers. How many flowers did Pat start with? Show your work?

???

Complete each number sentence to make it true.

4. $19 - 6 = 12$ 7. $4 + 7 = 11$

5. $12 – 7 = 4$ 8. $2 + 15 = 17$

6. $9 + 9 = 18$ 9. $18 - 6 = 11$

Figure 7.3 Beth's quiz.

Beth's math quiz and related post-assessment self-reflection showing that she answered six questions incorrectly (#1, #2, #3, #4, #5, #9), even though she only thought two of the problems (#1 and #3) were "hard" or that she didn't "know how to do it".

be very surprised and disappointed by her quiz results, but her teacher and parents should spend time explaining the different reasons she answered the questions incorrectly. Any teacher or parent who sees Beth's quiz score of 3/9 would probably conclude that she needs extra help; however, it is the post-assessment reflection that brings to light the fact that Beth did not even know she was misunderstanding the concepts. Based on her reflection, Beth thought she was prepared for the quiz.

_____Beth____'s Quiz Reflectionv

How do you think you did on the quiz?
Put a check in the area that describes how you feel about each question.

Question Number	This was easy	This was hard or I don't know how to do it
1		x
2	x	
3		x
4	x	
5	x	
6	x	
7	x	
8	x	
9	x	

Figure 7.3 (Continued)

Another very important takeaway for the teacher is the trend that both of these students, and likely many more, missed question #3 **and readily admitted that they did not understand what the question was asking or that it was hard**. The teacher would be wise to review this type of problem with all of her students since presumably so many of her students missed it and admitted that they need help with it. Whatever the reason—the teacher's delivery was ineffective, there was a schedule disruption/change and the content was not taught, etc.—several students did not master the material and are aware of it. It is the responsibility of the teachers, parents and students to fill in this gap of understanding.

8th Grade Quiz and Reflection

As students age and mature, the format of the assessments and the self-reflections may also change. Here we examine a sample 8th grade, four-question multiple choice quiz related to knowing and applying properties of integer exponents (CCSS.MATH.CONTENT.8.EE.A.1, http://www.corestandards. org/Math/Content/8/EE/A/1/).

This quiz (Figures 7.4(a and b)) is an example of something that may be given at the very end or beginning of a class to help the teacher, parents and student gauge student understanding. Quick assessments that only take a

Name _____ Date _____

Integer Exponent Quiz

CCSS.MATH.CONTENT.8.EE.A.1

Know and apply the properties of integer exponents to generate equivalent numerical expressions. For example, $3^2 \times 3^{-5} = 3^{-3} = 1/3^3 = 1/27$.

Pick the best answer for each question.

1. $3^5 = x$
   a. $x = 3$
   b. $x = 35$
   c. $x = 15$
   d. $x = 243$

2. $3^0 = x$
   a. $x = 0$
   b. $x = 1$
   c. $x = 3$
   d. $x = 9$

3. $4^4 \times 4^4$
   a. 4^8
   b. 4^{16}
   c. 16^4
   d. 16^8

4. $2^5 \times 2^3$
   a. 2^8
   b. 2^{15}
   c. 4^8
   d. 4^{15}

Figure 7.4 (a and b) 8th grade example.

A blank sample math quiz and related post-assessment self-reflection for an eighth grade math class.

_____'s Quiz Reflection

How do you think you did on the quiz?

Put a check in the area that describes how you feel about each question.

Question Number	No sweat!	This is hard/ confusing for me
1		
2		
3		
4		

Please write any other comments you have about the quiz here:

Figure 7.4 (Continued)

few minutes can be very valuable to all parties involved. The post-assessment self-reflection looks similar to the one given to 1st graders, not because 8th graders are incapable of diving deeper into metacognition—they most certainly are—but because this teacher may not want to spend more than a couple of minutes on this assessment and reflection. A similar cursory approach may be used at all grade levels, depending on time constraints and desired outcome. Asking students to categorize each question as "No sweat" (meaning, "I understand it") or "This is hard" forces students to decide one way or the other. They either feel very confident in their ability to answer the question or they don't. In this particular instance, the teacher wanted to only provide two options. On other assessments, she may provide a range of understanding level labels (i.e. *Circle a number between 1 and 5 to show how you feel about this question, 1 is "very confident" and 5 is "very confused"*). The teacher is usually best suited to make the decisions about the format and verbiage of the pre- and post-assessment student reflections, based on what information she is trying to glean.

A NOTE ABOUT THE QUESTIONS/OPTIONS YOU OFFER YOUR STUDENTS ON THE SELF-REFLECTIONS

Just as your classroom set-up, norms and teaching style say a lot about you as a teacher, so will your choice of length of and wording in the self-reflections. It is important that your students be crystal clear about what their choices for answering are, but it's really up to you what words you want to use. In the example with Ravi, the teacher uses "No sweat" to signify the option that the student completely understands the material. That might be an expression she uses with her students frequently. They should know very clearly that "No sweat" equates to "I understand." Other teachers may prefer to keep the self-reflections more formal with questions like, "I understand this question" or "I do not understand this question." Students in an English Learner program may not do well with slang or vernacular.

A teacher who wants a very quick look into students' introspection may only ask students about their level of understanding and not ask any further questions that may require more writing or thought.

Neither is better or worse; the choices you make in formatting and organizing the self-reflections are just one more way your personality as the teacher and the class's personalities may shine through. It's completely up to you. The words and length that you choose for the self-reflection are far less important than the information you gather from your students on them by setting up an environment where they can honestly reflect and then report.

Ravi's Quiz

Take a moment to review Ravi's multiple choice quiz first (Figure 7.5). He answered three out of four questions correctly; he only got #2 wrong. Based on the quiz alone, it appears that he seems to have mastered a good amount of the material. With no further information, Ravi's teacher would likely move on, truly believing that Ravi made one mistake on his quiz but mostly understands the material. At most, she would be able to ascertain that Ravi needed a quick review on what to do with numbers having an exponent of 0.

However, Ravi's 8th grade quiz and self-reflection is a great example of how this process can help reveal a "lucky guesser." Multiple choice/answer assessments are so valuable—and are often the format of standardized tests—and thus students need practice with them in their day-to-day classes. However, this format opens up the possibility that a student is a lucky guesser, and that results of their assessment do not accurately show their actual level of understanding. In Ravi's case, he only missed 1 of the 4 questions (#2). Without the self-reflection, his teacher and parents (and indeed Ravi himself) may believe that he has mastered the content. He looks as though he is ready to move on with minimal remediation and review only material related to numbers with exponents of zero.

However, when we look at the post-assessment reflection that he filled out before he turned in his test for grading (before he knew how he did on

Name _____ Ravi _____ Date _____

Integer Exponent Quiz

CCSS.MATH.CONTENT.8.EE.A.1

Know and apply the properties of integer exponents to generate equivalent numerical expressions. For example, $3^2 \times 3^{-5} = 3^{-3} = 1/3^3 = 1/27$.

Pick the best answer for each question.

1. $3^5 = x$
   a. $x = 3$
   b. $x = 35$
   c. $x = 15$
   d. $x = 243$

2. $3^0 = x$
   a. $x = 0$
   b. $x = 1$
   c. $x = 3$
   d. $x = 9$

3. $4^4 \times 4^4$
   a. 4^8
   b. 4^{16}
   c. 16^4
   d. 16^8

4. $2^5 \times 2^3$
   a. 2^8
   b. 2^{15}
   c. 4^8
   d. 4^{15}

Figure 7.5 (a and b) Ravi's quiz.

Ravi's 4-question math quiz and related post-assessment self-reflection. Ravi answered 3 out of the 4 questions correctly, so it would appear he only struggles with understanding one of the concepts. However, his self-reflection indicates that Ravi guessed luckily on each question of his quiz and that he desperately needs more instruction on exponents because he doesn't "get exponents at all" and all of the questions were "hard/confusing" for him.

_____Ravi__ 's Quiz Reflection

How do you think you did on the quiz?

Put a check in the area that describes how you feel about each question.

Question Number	No sweat!	This is hard/ confusing for me
1		✓
2		✓
3		✓
4		✓

Please write any other comments you have about the quiz here:

I don't get exponents at all.

Figure 7.5 (Continued)

each of the questions), we find something very, very different. He honestly admitted that he struggled with every single question. He was even so brave as to tell the teacher and his parents that he does not "get exponents at all." How wonderful that he was confident enough to be honest about his level of understanding! Now Ravi, the teacher and his parents know that he is struggling with all concepts related to exponents presented thus far, and that he needs help before moving on. Without this honest self-reflection, there is a chance that Ravi's teacher would begin introducing more complex material related to exponents, never knowing that Ravi was struggling with the fundamentals of exponents. **His quiz score alone seems to show that he is ready to move forward; however, his post-assessment reflection says something very different, and much more important.**

Even if Ravi knew he guessed on all of the questions, he may just feel like he will be able to move on in math without having to think about these concepts again. In classes without a post-assessment self-reflection, Ravi would likely be disinclined to mention any lack of understanding to teachers and parents. Why would he? He answered (really, guessed) three out of four questions correctly on his quiz. However, most teachers and parents (and some students) know that moving on from a topic before a student has a full understanding of it completely can lead to many problems in the subject area in the future. It is best to deal with misunderstanding at the time the subject matter is taught and evaluated, to repair any misunderstandings. Thankfully, the self-reflection provides an additional opportunity to discover students who are simply guessing, and encourages them to admit that they are struggling with understanding the content. Ravi's teacher is asking him to reflect on and record in writing his honest feelings about exponents. With this particular post-assessment reflection format, he can either 1) fib and say that he understands the concepts, or 2) take the opportunity—that might not otherwise be given to him if not for the post assessment reflection—to admit that he is still confused and needs more remediation. With practice and repeated positive reinforcement and outcomes, it should be clear to Ravi, his teacher and his parents that option #2 is the better one for him to choose.

8

Pre- and Post-Assessment Student Self-Reflections in English Language Arts (Writing and Reading)

Writing

While it may appear up until this point of the guide that the sciences, and in particular math, lend themselves most easily to demonstrate the value of pre- and post-assessment student self-reflections, that is simply not the case. There is so much valuable information to be gained when students, parents and teachers use pre- and post-assessment student self-reflections in all subject areas, at all grade levels.

In their article, "Self-Assessment in the Primary L2 Classroom" (2019), Wong and Mak conclude that there is great value in asking students to self-assess in writing classes, including students learning in their non-native language. They explain that "[o]ne primary purpose for self-assessment is for students to reflect on their writing and set tangible goals to improve their writing." Asking students to plan before writing is nothing new. Graphic organizers, outlines, webs, lists and charts are all integral parts of writing and are usually found in most effective classrooms. However, asking students to reflect on their writing abilities is a different task; one that is equally worthwhile. Before a writing assessment begins, teachers and parents should be asking the student to reflect on whether or not she understands the parts of the writing assessment, such as the correct integration of transitions or how to support a main idea with supporting details.

DOI: 10.4324/9781003329176-8

Wong and Mak (2019) illustrate the importance of pre- and post-assessment self-reflections in the writing classrooms by remarking that the:

> pre-writing stage is a critical time for self-assessment. It provides students time to reflect on their strengths and weaknesses, set goals, and consider how they will be assessed on their written work. The following are specific considerations for the classroom: Before beginning the writing process, teachers should make sure that all assessment criteria are clear to students. If students know the expectations of their written products, they can create goals that are tangible, achievable, objective, and, most importantly, easy to self-assess. In addition, educators should ensure that assessment criteria are available and that the language used in assessment criteria is accessible to students.

The process that Wong and Mak describe is similar to the pre- and post-assessment self-reflections described in this guide.

Furthermore, in their study exploring "the relationship between self-assessment, planning and goal setting, and reflection on self-efficacy in student writing by having students use a revision planner as part of their writing process during a strategy-based reading and writing intervention", Chung et al. (2021) make clear that encouraging students to reflect using a "planner" is an important tool for improving their writing. They explain that "[unlike] a rubric, a planner focuses students' attention on actionable steps that they can take to reach specific goals that they can set for themselves—based upon what they have learned throughout the intervention- to help them manage their revision process and revise their writing successfully." Chung and his colleagues hypothesized that having students fill out a "planner" (a form of a pre-assessment student self-reflection), in which "students participate in assessing their own strengths and areas for improvement as writing and fill out a reflection similar to the one their teachers created would lead to better writing outcomes." Based on their results, Chung et al. (2021) concluded that "engaging students in assessing their own strengths and areas for growth and then reflecting on their progress can enhance students' motivation and commitment."

Additionally, they note in their paper that the process of pre-assessment student reflection is most valuable when teachers are also involved. If teachers can analyze the pre-assessment student self-reflections to determine trends in student misunderstanding and build intervention lessons into the days leading up to the assessment, students will likely benefit. For example, if a teacher sees on Tuesday afternoon that many of her students struggled to clearly show mastery of "using transition words" on the pre-assessment student self-reflection (see below), a good use of Wednesday's or Thursday's direct instruction time would be a thorough review of transition words and their implementation. Then, by assessment day (presumably Friday of that same week), students should be more equipped to include transition words in their writing assessment.

With that in mind, I believe if parents are willing and able to help their child identify and remediate a writing objective that is unclear, the child would benefit. For instance, if a parent sees his 4th grade son's pre-assessment self-reflection has revealed that the student does not understand how to organize his thoughts with a main idea and supporting details, the parent can either offer an intervention directly, or notify his son's teacher and ask that the teacher help build more understanding of the confusing concept.

For example, if the assessment will be having the student plan, write and revise a persuasive essay, a sample pre-assessment self-reflection in writing might look similar to this template (Figure 8.1).

Concept or Sample Question	DO YOU UNDERSTAND THIS CONCEPT?	
* I understand how to introduce claim(s) and organize the reasons and evidence clearly.	YES -------->	Explain:
	NO, but I am going to do this to help my understanding	use a graphic organizer ask my teacher, friend or family member review past writing projects/ examples other: _____ _____
* I understand how use appropriate transitions to clarify the relationships among ideas and concepts.	YES -------->	Explain:
	NO, but I am going to do this to help my understanding	Review past assignments/ mini-lessons ask my teacher, friend or family member find examples of transition words in my book & review how they are used other: _____ _____
* I know how to provide a concluding statement or section that follows from the argument presented.	YES -------->	Explain:
	NO, but I am going to do this to help my understanding	Review past assignments/ notes ask my teacher, friend or family member watch a video about concluding statements other: _____ _____

Figure 8.1 Sample pre-assessment self-reflection in writing.

In this example, students would be given the pre-assessment template several days before the essay is to be written so they can reflect on their level of understanding. For instance, do they list that transitions are needed to make relationships between ideas or words more clear, and can they list words like "next, then, however, for example, finally…"? For the third question about the parts of an essay, can they fill in that their essay needs to include an introduction, x number of supporting reasons and a conclusion? Another option would be to give students a sample essay that includes examples of each of these objectives and ask students to identify them either by highlighting them in a certain color, rewriting them onto the self-assessment reflection, or even physically cutting and pasting from the exemplar onto the correct area of the reflection to demonstrate understanding and mastery.

If teachers review the pre-assessment reflection and find that their students do not have solid lists of transitions, or recognize the essential parts of an essay, the next few writing classes should be dedicated to filling in those holes. Parents who are able to review the pre-assessment writing reflection and guide their children would also be assets.

Once the students are asked to begin the actual essay writing, a sample template that resembles a detailed checklist might be given to them (Figure 8.2). This would be given to the students while they are planning, writing and revising their essay—but before they turn in the essay for teacher review.

A student would then fill out this quick reflection and attach it to the essay for the teacher to review. If the teacher notes that the child did not use any transitions in the essay, but sees that he marked "Yes" next to that reflection point, the teacher should note that there is a disconnect. The child still may not understand what a transition is, when to use one or what its purpose is. In any event, the child felt like he did use transitions, which means he would be unlikely to ask for clarification in the future. It would be important for the teacher or parent to initiate a conversation about transitions with the child since he believes he uses them properly.

	Yes	I don't know	Thoughts/Questions?
I organized my essay properly			
I used transitions thoughtfully.			
I included the essential parts of an essay.			

Figure 8.2 Writing checklist.

A simple post-assessment self-reflection template that may be given to students after they write an essay, but before they turn it in for evaluation.

CAN'T I JUST KEEP USING A RUBRIC TO ASSESS MY STUDENTS' WRITING?

Absolutely! Please keep using a rubric. The value of a rubric is not diminished by the addition of student self-reflections.

It is important to note that the teacher's chosen method of assessing the essay—often a writing rubric—is still pertinent and helpful. The value of a scoring rubric is not undermined in any way by these pre- and post-assessment reflections. The reflections are meant to help the student think about his level of understanding, and to uncover any disconnect between student performance and actual student understanding. Chung and colleagues explain that the self-reflection ("planner" in their words) shares some similarities to a traditional writing rubric, but offers multitudes of valuable information and opportunity to intervene before an assessment even takes place that a rubric may not. Chung et al. (2021) state:

> Like a rubric (Andrade et al., 2010), a planner can serve as a tool to support students in revising and improving their work. Unlike a rubric, a planner focuses students' attention on actionable steps that they can take to reach specific goals that they can set for themselves—based upon what they have learned throughout the intervention—to help them manage their revision process and review their writing successfully.

For example, if the student did not use transitions, but marked that he "used transitions thoughtfully," the teacher would still need to give him a "0" on the scoring rubric, but would gain helpful insight that the lack of transitions wasn't an oversight. The student believes that he used transitions when he clearly did not. In this instance, what the child said he did (use transitions) and what he actually did (omitted transitions) uncovered a discrepancy between student understanding and student performance. It would be helpful for the teacher, parent and student to dig deeper to find out why the student did not use transitions yet marked that he did. Did he confuse the concept of transition words with something like indentations? Did he put commas after the third word in each sentence believing that made his essay have transition words? The possibilities are endless, but determining why the student did and said different things is paramount to fixing the problem.

We can now take a closer look at sample pre-assessment self-reflection that Susie filled out several days prior to her writing assessment (Figure 8.3).

Based on this pre-assessment self-reflection, it appears that Susie understands that she needs to select one argument and provide support for

Concept or Sample Question	DO YOU UNDERSTAND THIS CONCEPT?	
* I understand how to introduce claim(s) and organize the reasons and evidence clearly.	YES ------->	Explain: I will pick only one side that I agree with and add 3 sentences to each paragraph to show why it is the best.
	NO, but I am going to do this to help my understanding	use a graphic organizer ask my teacher, friend or family member review past writing projects/ examples other: _____ _____
* I understand how use appropriate transitions to clarify the relationships among ideas and concepts.	YES ---------->	Explain:
	NO, but I am going to do this to help my understanding	Review past assignments/ mini-lessons ask my teacher, friend or family member find examples of transition words in my book & review how they are used other: _____ _____
* I know how to provide a concluding statement or section that follows from the argument presented.	YES ------->	Explain: Yep, I will say my side again at the end of the paragraphs.
	NO, but I am going to do this to help my understanding	Review past assignments/ notes ask my teacher, friend or family member watch a video about concluding statements other: _____ _____

Figure 8.3 Susie's pre-assessment self-reflection.

it. She appears to understand that she also needs to include a conclusion. What she has shared with her teacher and perhaps parents, however, is that she does not completely understand how to use transitions in her writing. Through pre-assessment reflection, she has identified a goal (*to understand how to use appropriate transitions to clarify the relationships among ideas and concepts*) and an action plan (*ask my teacher, friend or family member*) to get necessary intervention.

If there are several students in Susie's class who are also discovering upon reflection that they do not have a firm grasp on using transition words, the teacher would be wise to spend at least one of the remaining class days before the assessment reviewing transitions. Whether it is a whole-group, small-group or one-on-one meeting depends on how many of the students need remediation, as well as other factors like class size, teacher ratios and how many other areas of content need to be reviewed before the assessment.

Based on her pre-assessment reflection plan, a day or so after she completed the reflection, but before assessment day, Susie should have asked a trusted adult for more help with implementing transitions. Ideally, she would then return to the pre-assessment reflection and complete it by giving examples of how she mastered the concept.

Figure 8.4 (a and b) is an example of Susie's essay assessment as well as the post-assessment self-reflection that she fills out before turning in the essay for evaluation:

Did you know, that 90% of artificial Christmas Trees are shipped from China and end up in landfills? Artificial trees hurt the environment. I believe that people should buy real Christmas Trees because they give people jobs, they are better for the environment, and they are unique.

Real Christmas trees, create jobs and money for people. Did you know, that there are close to 15,000 Christmas tree farms in the U.S. and more than 100,000 people work there? These farms provide jobs and money for tons of people! If you buy an artificial Christmas tree, you're essentially taking away and not supporting the employees there.

Artificial Christmas trees, are very bad for the environment. Artificial trees are shipped over from different countries and just one of these trees take 2,700 years to decompose! 75,000,000 Christmas trees are bought every year. That basically means people who buy artificial trees are hurting the environment. Real Christmas trees help the environment and fight global warming.

Real Christmas trees, are just unique. Knowing that the Christmas tree in your house grew in the ground among thousands that each look different is special. When you buy an artificial tree that looks identical to hundreds more out there, it just isn't the same. Even though real Christmas trees are a bit of work, it's well worth it to have the fresh scent and the feeling of a real Christmas.

This Christmas, go to a local farm and chop down a real tree for your house. Not only does it support the employees there, but their very unique and artificial Christmas trees hurt the environment. I hope you decide to buy a real Christmas tree this year and enjoy the experience!

(a)

Figure 8.4 (a) Sample writing piece. (b) post-assessment self-reflection.

A sample writing piece used with permission (the author's daughter) to demonstrate the value of the post-assessment reflection template, simple though it may be. We can glean from the reflection that Susie believes she used transitions in her persuasive writing because she used commas. Because of how she answered her reflection, her teacher can be sure that she did not forgot to use transition words - which might be a natural conclusion, given all of the aspects of writing students are asked to consider when planning, writing, revising and completing a writing piece.

	Yes	I don't know	Thoughts/Questions?
I organized my essay properly	×		
I used transitions thoughtfully.	×		I used commas.
I included the essential parts of an essay.	×		

(b)

Figure 8.4 (Continued)

Comparing Susie's essay with her post-assessment self-reflection shows us that Susie believes that by using commas, she used transitions. Sure enough, she did include commas at the beginning of each paragraph after two or three words; however, the words that she used were not transitions. Her essay, coupled with the post-assessment student self-reflection, show that, even with a review of transition words, Susie is struggling with the concept and its implementation. It appears that somewhere along the way—even after extra help—she internalized that there are usually commas before or after transition words, but did not understand the idea that transition words should be used to connect ideas or show sequence. She would likely benefit from yet another review of transition words and their use, as well as a review on commas. A fresh new approach is likely needed since she does not seem to understand transitions even after two or more attempts to review transitions. This process would be a great indicator that the teacher's current method of introducing transitions is not resonating with Susie or any other students still struggling with them. The teacher would do well to reflect on her own teaching methods and examples to see if she can determine why the students are still not mastering the concept.

Since there are so many writing skills that we ask students to demonstrate in an assessment, the post-assessment reflection confirms that the lack of transitions in Susie's essay was not an oversight. She did not get overwhelmed with all of the other facets of good writing that we often ask our students to incorporate—punctuation, spelling, capitalization, indentation and support of the main ideas, etc.—and simply forget to include transitions. Rather, the post-assessment student self-reflection shows that she believes that she did include transitions in her essay because she included commas, and, as a result, she would benefit from further instruction.

Reading

In his article, Peter Afflerbach (2016) states:

> [a] major goal of reading instruction is fostering the development of independent, successful student readers. To be independent and successful, all readers must assume responsibility for self-assessment: setting clear goals for reading, monitoring progress along the reading path, and determining if reading is successful. All independent readers self-assess, but self-assessment is not always the focus of reading assessment. It must be.

He continues later by saying that "we can encourage students to look first to themselves to answer questions that include 'How am I doing?' 'Is there a problem' 'What is it?' 'How can I fix the problem?' and 'How am I progressing toward my reading goal(s)?'" (Afflerbach, 2016).

Piggybacking off of Afflerbach's claims, I would posit that a pre-assessment self-reflection related to reading would not only help the student become a better independent reader, but also uncover what the teacher (and perhaps parents) need to do to help the student improve. In their article about student self-assessment, Chung et al. (2021) head off opponents who sometimes use the argument that giving students similar problems or writing samples in advance of the post-assessments creates an unfair advantage. They state, "[t] o avoid 'teaching to the test', teachers use a different text, but similar in topic as the text used for the writing assessment as a training tool in order to model how to review the pre-test into a multiple draft essay." The same should be done in the reading classroom.

For example, if the goal of the reading unit in the 4th grade is to *determine the main idea of a text and explain how it is supported by key details; summarize the text* (CCSS.ELA-LITERACY.RI.4.2; http://www.corestandards. org/ELA-Literacy/RI/4/2/), it would be perfectly acceptable and very beneficial to all parties involved (student, parent and teacher) to present the students with a sample reading passage that is similar to the one to be used on the post-assessment, and a pre-assessment student self-reflection like the one below (Figure 8.5) a few days before the reading assessment is to take place.

For example, if the reading assessment is to take place on Friday, the teacher may present this pre-assessment self-reflection and a sample passage to the students on Monday afternoon for homework. The students turn in the completed paper Tuesday, giving the students two more class periods

Concept or Sample Question	DO YOU UNDERSTAND THIS CONCEPT?	
* I can determine the main idea of the text.	YES --------->	Explain what the main idea is here:
	NO, but I am going to do this to help my understanding	re-read the title to look for hints ask my teacher, friend or family memberto explain main ideas look at the first couple, and last couple sentences other: _____ _____
* I can find supporting details for the main idea.	YES --------->	List 2-3 supporting details:
	NO, but I am going to do this to help my understanding	Underline the main idea and look for details that are related ask my teacher, friend or family member use a graphic organizer other: _____ _____
* I can summarize the text.	YES --------->	Give a 2-3 sentence summary of the text:
	NO, but I am going to do this to help my understanding	Review past assignments/ mini-lessons ask my teacher, friend or family member Underline important information/facts other: _____ _____

Figure 8.5 Pre-assessment self-reflection.

to get any necessary intervention. If the students are willing to advocate for themselves about the weaknesses they may have realized when completing the self-assessment, they can ask for focused lessons and additional help from the teacher or parents on, for example, finding the main idea. Otherwise, the teachers can use Tuesday afternoon to review the student self-assessments and plan appropriate lessons in whole-group, small-group or individual settings. If there are enough students struggling with one or more of the concepts, the teacher can use that as an opportunity to reexamine her method of content delivery. Where is the disconnect between what she was trying to teach, and what the students did/not grasp? If there are just a handful of students struggling with each of the concepts, perhaps stations or centers would be a better fit for the classroom.

Whatever the intervention method the teacher chooses to be most appropriate, the most important takeaway is the students recognized their own lack of understanding **before** the assessment took place, leaving time for the teacher to intervene, and giving her students the best chance at mastering the content before the assessment. Rather than taking a test on Friday and having student, teacher and parents potentially be surprised by the results, the pre-assessment self-reflection allows the students to think about and reflect on their own understanding at a time when there is still time to correct the problem or clarify the misunderstanding.

When the day of the assessment arrives, student, teacher, and parent should feel more confident in the student's ability to show mastery of the objectives that were presented in the pre-assessment self-reflection, and worked on in the days leading up to the post-assessment. In keeping with the example stated earlier, it would be helpful for the teacher to present a post-test student self-assessment for the student to complete after completing the assessment but **before** turning in the assessment.

It could be as simple as a chart like Figure 8.6.

Now, with the post-assessment student self-reflection in hand, the teacher can compare how the child *thinks* he did on the assessment with how he *actually* did on the assessment. If the student marked that he did not find, or did not know if he found, the main idea, but had correctly underlined the main idea, the teacher can be fairly certain the child guessed on the answer.

Circle how you feel you did on this assignment. Fill this out before you turn in your paper to me!			
I found the main idea of the passage.	**YES**	**I DON'T KNOW**	**NO**
I found supporting details.	**YES**	**I DON'T KNOW**	**NO**
I summarized the text.	**YES**	**I DON'T KNOW**	**NO**
What was easy for you? _____			
What was hard for you? _____			

Figure 8.6 Post-test self-assessment.

A simple post-assessment reflection template that may help students and teacher best reflect on the student's level of understanding of the target reading concepts, as well as what the student believes she has mastered ("easy") and with what concepts she may still be struggling ("hard").

This would be a call for further intervention and review. Without this post-assessment, the teacher might assume that the child has full understanding of main idea when really it was just a lucky guess.

As evidenced by many researchers and educators, incorporating student self-reflection in writing and reading classrooms is a process that is beneficial to parents and teachers, but, most importantly, to students. Students should be given opportunities and coaching on how to reflect on their own under-standing and ability to demonstrate mastery of the set objectives, make action plans, complete the task or assessment and then reflect again on their abil-ity. This process gives teachers, parents and the students themselves ample opportunity to identify misconceptions and correct them, in a timeline that limits stress and maximizes learning.

9

Putting It All Together

In summary, student self-reflections—completed both before and after students have taken the assessments—can prove enormously helpful to teachers, parents and the students themselves. Asking students to reflect on their level of understanding at different times in their learning evolution can help teachers, parents and students determine which students have mastered the concept(s) and which students still need more instruction and/or remediation. Teachers can use the pre- and post-student self-reflections to make whole-class generalizations about the efficacy of their own teaching style, materials and presentation, as well as determine which specific students need which help with particular concepts. Andrade and Valtcheva (2009) found that students themselves quickly saw the value in self-assessment. "Students said that criteria-referenced self-assessment helped them focus on key elements of an assignment, learn the material, increase their effectiveness in identifying strengths and weaknesses of their work, increase their motivation and mindfulness, and even decrease anxiety."

DOI: 10.4324/9781003329176-9

Benefits of Pre- and Post-Assessment Student Self-Reflections for the Student, Teacher, and Parent:

STUDENT

Pre-Assessment Self-Reflections

◆ Clearly outlines the desired objectives and goals asked of the student
◆ Helps determine student's own strengths and weaknesses related to particular concepts
◆ Asks student to demonstrate mastery, rather than studying without requiring proof of understanding
◆ Asks student to create and execute a plan of action that he feels will best suit his needs based on learning style, content, time frame, resources available, etc.

Post-Assessment Self-Reflections

◆ Encourages students to reflect on their perceived level of understanding before knowing definitively if they answered the question/demonstrated mastery correctly
◆ Encourages students to check their own work as students must review and rate understanding of concepts/problems before turning the assessment in for evaluation

---

TEACHER

Pre-Assessment Self-Reflections

◆ Gives teacher the opportunity to gauge individual student understanding days/classes before an evaluation
◆ Gives teacher enough time to provide intervention and remediation, or extensions if needed
◆ Gives teacher flexibility to change assessment date to either extend or shorten teaching days based on individual and class trends, maximizing valuable class time
◆ Gives teacher tangible evidence of effectiveness of her presentation of material based on individual and whole-class trends

Post-Assessment Self-Reflections

◆ Helps teacher identify concepts that still elude individual students or entire groups of students

◆ Allows teacher to find "lucky guessers" if student revealed she did not understand question but answered it correctly
◆ Allows teacher to place emphasis on value of students checking and correcting their own work before it is turned in for evaluation
◆ Allows teacher to evaluate her own method of teacher, resources used to determine effectiveness based on student reflections and assessment outcomes

PARENT/CAREGIVER

Pre-Assessment Self-Reflections

◆ Clearly outlines desired objectives toward which the students are working
◆ Provides valuable information about individual student understanding
◆ Allows parent to be an integral part of child's learning journey
◆ Gives parent time to help child before an evaluation in an environment that may be less stressful
◆ Gives parent time to contact child's teacher for additional resources or insights

Post-Assessment Self-Reflections

◆ Allows parent to gain insight into child's level of conceptual understanding at the time of assessment
◆ Allows parent the opportunity to offer additional assistance if possible

Overview of the Sequence for Including Pre- and Post-Assessment Self-Reflections

Weeks Leading Up to Assessment Day: Teacher presents desired learning objectives and outcomes to students and parents, and teaches material with those objectives in mind

Approximately 4–5 class periods before Assessment Day: Teacher presents an appropriately structured and designed "Pre-Assessment Student Self-Reflection" to each student and has them complete it. Teachers use similar, **but not the same**, problems/objectives that will be on the assessment. During this time, the students see the concepts on which they will be assessed and are asked to reflect on their level of understanding for each. If they feel strongly that they understand the particular concept, they "prove" their understanding by filling out the pre-assessment self-reflection with words, numbers, pictures, etc. If they feel as though the need more help or do not have a firm grasp on the concept, they must come up with an action plan (ask a teacher/trusted adult/peer for help, review direct instruction notes, watch an approved video, visit an approved website, play a game, etc.), complete the action plan and then fill out the pre-assessment reflection drawing on their understanding gleaned from the intervention.

Approximately 1–3 class periods before Assessment Day: During this time, the teacher and parents review the students' reflections. The teacher makes necessary adjustment to lessons, determining which students need remediation and which students are ready for enrichment. If a large group of students is struggling with one particular concept, the teacher should be reflecting on his delivery and choice of materials/assignments to determine the cause of the mass confusion. The parents (whenever possible) are also supporting their child at home, or by contacting the teacher to make them aware of confusion and/or ask for advice/additional resources on how best to support their child.

Assessment Day: Students take the assessment, and then **before turning it in for evaluation**, complete the post-assessment self-reflection. At this point, the student has completed the assessment, but does not yet know how he did on it (i.e. the assessment has not been graded/evaluated). The student reflects on each specific question, answering how confident he is on his mastery of the concept. Depending on the concept being assessed, age and ability of students, the teacher may also ask more broad questions about the "most challenging" or "easiest" parts of the test, or if the student was able to review his work and find any mistakes that needed correcting.

Approximately 1–3 days after Assessment Day: Teacher reviews the assessments, as well as the post-assessment self-reflections, and makes connections between the two, as best as possible. The teacher may be looking for students who answered question types correctly, but marked that they do not understand the concept ("lucky guessers"). The teacher may also be looking at students who answered the questions incorrectly, but marked that they thought they had mastered the material, as this may indicate that the student would not choose to get additional assistance, as they do not know that they have not correctly demonstrated mastery. Then the teacher determines the need for further instruction in class. Ideally, the teacher is also able to loop in the individual students and their parents to share the information and offer suggestion for extracurricular remediation ideas, if needed and possible.

Days/Months after Assessment: Student, teacher and parents can use the pre- and post-assessment student self-reflections to review content that been mastered earlier in the year, either for the purpose of studying for end-of-year assessments, or as a reminder of concepts (and mastery or misunderstanding thereof) that the student had at different times in the year, and the actions that were taken to help ensure mastery of the material.

Frequently Asked Questions (FAQ)

Isn't this a lot of extra work for the teacher(s)?

It will take a bit of getting used to, but creating pre- and post-assessment self-reflections can be done very quickly, assuming the unit objectives are clearly stated and outlined from the beginning. The teacher simply lists the objectives or sample problems for the students (and parents) to see in advance of the assessment. Reviewing each student's pre- and post-assessments should not take more than 1–2 minutes, and the benefit of doing so may save a large amount of precious class time. Using the information from the reflections can help teachers know exactly which students need help with exactly which concepts. No longer will the teachers be re-teaching material that students already know. Also, if teachers can use post-assessment reflections to determine that they need to spend more time on a foundational unit before moving on to a more complex unit that builds on the preceding one, they will no doubt save time in the long run. If students' foundational understanding is shaky, there is little reason to move on.

Aren't my students too old/young for this, or incapable of doing this because of a learning difference?

The pre- and post-assessment student reflections should be catered to the students' age and ability, no doubt. Younger students or students who have learning differences that impact their ability to read or write, for example, may do better with reflections that are more picture-based or simpler in format. Older students, even those in high school or college level, should have reflections that ask them to perhaps "dig deeper" or show more mastery. Each teacher's reflections might look different for each unit that they teach.

Just as you collaborate with the Special Education, English Learner, Gifted Talented or other specialists on creating appropriate content and assessments, so too should you team up with them on the student self-reflections. Consider implementing the same or similar accommodations and modifications on the reflections that you do for your special needs students typically. Allowing students to reflect orally (rather than in writing), extending the time allotted, reading the material aloud, etc. can all be applied to the self-reflections as well.

How do I get started?

Start small and start with reflections that ask students about topics that they enjoy and/or ones in which feel confident. Refer to the chapter in this guide where there is an example of a project that students are asked to complete that might be viewed as "off-topic" but would allow students to focus on whether or not they understood the objective before starting the project (a version of the pre-assessment self-reflection) and then create an action plan, if not. In this example the students then also self-reflect on their competency at completing the finished project (a version of the post-assessment self-reflection). Another great way to introduce the routine of self-reflection would be to have simple questions after or next to each assessment question, asking your students to rate how they think they did on that particular question (i.e. circle whether this question was "easy" or "hard").

Once students start to feel confident in their ability to honestly and accurate assess their own level of understanding and mastery, it may be appropriate to add more detail/questions/prompts to the pre- and post-assessment self-reflections to ask your students to look inward at their progress and comprehension of the target objectives even more.

Is self-reflection really beneficial to students?

Teacher researcher and college professor Kathleen Hickey reported that when she asked her college-level students to try self-reflection as part of an assessment, she was shocked by their responses. She explains:

What I was not ready for was that my students reported that they had no experience whatsoever in doing such self-reflection. *All* of them claimed that throughout their educational histories, they had never been asked to think about themselves or how they learned. (Hickey, 2009)

We, as teachers and parents, have to do better for our students. Instilling the habit of self-reflection in our students early in their educational lives can help our students immeasurably—first as students, then as professionals and contributing members of society. The long-term benefits of making self-reflection a habit have been well documented. Driessen, van Tartwijk, and Dornan (2008) explain that, "[a]ll UK doctors are now expected to make reflection a critical foundation of their lifelong learning (General Medical Council, 2000) on the assumption that patients will benefit" (General Medical Council, 2003). They continue "[s]tudents do not adopt reflective learning habits spontaneously (Ertmer and Newby, 1996), so teachers must help them." Given the many benefits and applications of self-reflection, it should have a place in every classroom and should be taught and practiced regularly.

Appendix
Sample Pre- and Post-Assessment Student Reflection Formats and Uses

Sample Pre-Assessment Student Self-Reflection Templates

Pre-Assessment Student Self-Reflection Template

Pre-Assessment Student Self-Reflection Template

Concept or Sample Question	DO YOU UNDERSTAND THIS CONCEPT?		
*Sample Question #1	YES ---------->	Explain:	
	NO, but I am going to do this to help my understanding	Review past assignments/ notes Draw picture	ask my teacher or family member other: _____ _____
*Sample Question #2	YES ---------->	Explain:	
	NO, but I am going to do this to help my understanding	Play a game related to this Watch an approved video	ask a friend or family member other: _____ _____

Name _____

	I have got it!	I need a little more time.
I know the letter ___.	☐ 😄	☐ 🕒
My words match the picture.	☐ 😄	☐ 🕒
I can read this back to you.	☐ 😄	☐ 🕒

Sample Post-Assessment Student Self-Reflections

Name _____   Date   _____

Assessment Reflection

Put a check next to each number that describes how you feel about it.
Remember, this is between you and me; be honest.

Question Number	It is Very Easy	I Feel Pretty Good About This	I Could Use Some More Help	I Need A LOT More Help	I Have No Idea What the Question is Asking of Me
1.					
2.					
3.					
4.					
5.					
6.					
7.					
8.					
9.					
10.					
11.					
12.					
13.					

What part of the test did you think was easiest?
_____
_____
_____

What part of the test was the hardest for you?
_____
_____
_____

You should have checked your work before turning it in. Please tell me which numbers, if any, you were able to correct because you checked your work.

_____

_____

_____

Name _____

	I have got it!	I need a little more time.
I know the letter ___.	☐ 😄	☐ 🕐
My words match the picture.	☐ 😄	☐ 🕐
I can read this back to you.	☐ 😄	☐ 🕐

Name _____ Date_____

Quiz Reflection

Describe each quiz question, using a 1, 2, 3 or 4. Remember, this is between you and me; be honest.

1-Easy	2-Medium	3-Hard	4-Super Hard

Question 1 _____
Question 2 _____
Question 3 _____
Question 4 _____
Question 5 _____
Question 6 _____
Question 7 _____

What did you do to make sure you got the correct answers?
_____
_____

What problems did you find the most challenging? Why?
_____
_____

What can you do to help you on the problems you struggled with?
_____
_____
_____
_____

Some teachers, parents and/or students may prefer to have the reflection immediately following each assessment item or at the bottom of each assessment page (after a couple of assessment questions). An example of the former might be:

1. *Assessment Item Here*

	Circle the choice that best describes how you felt about answering the question above:		
STOP	Question 1 was:	EASY	HARD, BUT I THINK I GOT IT	I GUESSED

2. *Assessment Item Here*

	Circle the choice that best describes how you felt about answering the question above:		
STOP	Question 2 was:	EASY	HARD, BUT I THINK I GOT IT	I GUESSED

An example of the reflection being at the bottom of each assessment page:

Assessment Item #1
Assessment Item #2
Assessment Item #3

	Circle the choice that best describes how you felt about answering the questions 1-3 above:		
STOP	These questions were:	EASY	HARD, BUT I THINK I GOT IT	I GUESSED

Your preference and your students' preferences for collecting data may vary. Here are even more suggestions for additional questions/opportunities for students to reflect on and share their level of understanding:

- I (do or do not) understand this question/concept. [Circle one]
- Which question/concept could you confidently teach to another student in our class?
- Which question/concept would you want a classmate to review with you?
- Rank the questions in order from 1–x, based on how well you know the material. (1 is for the questions that you know best and x is for the ones that you are least confident about).

- ◆ Which of the following describes how you feel about #*x*?
  - ◆ ___ very good
  - ◆ ___ a little confused
  - ◆ ___ very confused
  - ◆ ___ I do not understand this

- ◆ Mark on the scale how you feel about this question/concept:

I completely understand

this concept

I am really struggling

with this

- ◆ Which picture shows how you feel about this question/concept (circle one):

easy   so-so   totally-confusing

> I've found that sometimes students will respond more honestly if they can circle a picture to indicate how they are feeling, rather than having to write out or circle words that mean the same thing. This is especially true with younger students.

- ◆ Which question was the easiest for you and why? Which question was the most challenging?
- ◆ Could you teach someone (your friend, parent) how to solve questions 1–3? Are there any questions you wouldn't feel comfortable teaching someone else? Which ones?
- ◆ Did you double-check your work? Did you find any mistakes that you were able to correct? Which numbers and what were the mistakes?
- ◆ Are there any questions on this assessment that you never want to see again? Which ones and why?

Works Cited

Afflerbach, P. (2016). Reading assessment: Looking ahead. *The Reading Teacher*, 69(4), 413–419.

Andrade, H.G., & Valtcheva, A.V. (2009). Promoting learning and achievement through self-assessment. *Theory Into Practice*, 48, 12–19.

Andrade, H.L., Du, Y., & Mycek, K. (2010). Rubric-referenced self-assessment and middle school students' writing. *Assessment in Education: Principles, Policy & Practice*, 17(2), 199–214.

Bercher, D.A. (2012). Self-monitoring tools and student academic success: When perception matches reality. *The Journal of College Science Teaching*, 41, 26–32.

Blackwell, L.S., Trzesniewski, K.H., & Dweck, C.S. (2007). Implicit theories of intelligence predict achievement across an adolescent transition: A longitudinal study and an intervention. *Child Development*, 78(1), 246–263.

Bozan, S. (2021). Determining students' reflective thinking levels and examining their reflections on science concepts. *African Educational Research Journal*, 9(2), 544–550.

Chung, H.Q., Chen, V., & Olson, C.B. (2021). The impact of self-assessment, planning and goal setting, and reflection before and after revision on student self-efficacy and writing performance. *Reading and Writing*, 34, 1885–1913.

Driessen, E., van Tartwijk, J., & Dornan, T. (2008). The self critical doctor: Helping students become more reflective. *BMJ*, 336(7648), 827–830. https://doi.org/10.1136/bmj.39503.608032.AD

Ehrlinger, J., Johnson, K., Banner, M., Dunning, D., & Kruger, J. (2008). Why the unskilled are unaware: Further explorations of (absent) self-insight among the incompetent. *Organizational Behavior and Human Decision Processes*, 105(1), 98–121. https://doi.org/10.1016/j.obhdp.2007.05.002

Ertmer, P.A., Newby, T.J. (1996). The expert learner: Strategic, self-regulated, and reflective. *Instructional Science* 24, 1–24. https://doi.org/10.1007/BF00156001

General Medical Council (2000). *Revalidating doctors: Ensuring standards, securing the future*. London: GMC.

General Medical Council (2003). Tomorrow's doctors: Recommendations on undergraduate medical education. www.gmc-uk.org/education/undergraduate/undergraduate_policy/tomorrows_doctors.asp

Hacker, D.J., Bol, L., Horgan, D.D., & Rakow, E.A. (2000). Test prediction and performance in a classroom context. *Journal of Educational Psychology*, 92, 160–170.

Herman, J.L. (1992). What research tells us about good assessment. *Educational Leadership*, 49(8), 74–78.

Hickey, K. (2009). A self-reflective view of reading assessment. *Research and Teaching in Developmental Education*, 26(1), 58–67. http://www.jstor.org/stable/42802342

Hill, M. (1995). Self assessment in primary schools: A response to student teacher questions. *Waikato Journal of Education*, (1), 61–70.

Johansson, S. The relationship between students' self-assessed reading skills and other measures of achievement. *Large-scale Assessments in Education* 1, 3 (2013). https://doi.org/10.1186/2196-0739-1-3

Kuncel, N.R., Credé, M., & Thomas, L.L.. (2005). The validity of self-reported grade point averages, class ranks, and test scores: A meta-analysis. *Review of Educational Research*, 75(1), 63–82.

McDonald, B. (2007). Self assessment for understanding. *The Journal of Education*, 188(1), 25–40. http://www.jstor.org/stable/42744121

McMillan, J.H., & Hearn, J. (2008). Student self-assessment: The key to stronger student motivation and higher achievement. *Educational Horizons*, 87(1), 40–49. http://www.jstor.org/stable/42923742

McPherson, G.E., & Renwick, J.M. (2011). Self-regulation and mastery of musical skills. In B.J. Zimmerman, & D.H. Schunk (Eds.), *Handbook of self-regulation of learning and performance* (pp. 234–248). New York: Routledge/Taylor & Francis Group.

Oscarson, A.D. (2009). Self-assessment of writing in learning English as a foreign language: A study at the upper secondary school level. *Goteborg Studies in Educational Sciences*, 277.

Stallings, V., & Tascoine, C. (1996). Student self-assessment and self-evaluation. *The Mathematics Teacher*, 89(7), 548–554. http://www.jstor.org/stable/27969906

Valle, C., Andrade, H., Palma, M., & Hefferen, J. (2016). Applications of peer assessment and self-assessment in music. *Music Educators Journal*, 102(4), 41–49. http://www.jstor.org/stable/24755680

Wong, K.M., & Mak, P. (2019). Self-assessment in the primary L2 writing classroom. *The Canadian Modern Language Review/La revue canadienne des langues vivantes*, 75, 183–196.

Woods, D.R. (1987). Student self-performance assessment. *Journal of College Science Teaching*, 16(6), 565–570. http://www.jstor.org/stable/42987324

For Product Safety Concerns and Information please contact our EU
representative GPSR@taylorandfrancis.com
Taylor & Francis Verlag GmbH, Kaufingerstraße 24, 80331 München, Germany

www.ingramcontent.com/pod-product-compliance
Ingram Content Group UK Ltd.
Pitfield, Milton Keynes, MK11 3LW, UK
UKHW031041080625
459435UK00013B/574